$49.00

Venus Legacy $149.00

☆ Velashape

☆ Fat Splitting System – ~~Duty~~ Beauty Dom

☆ Cool Sculpting

Fat Free

BECOMING EVER *Mindful*

DAVID J. SACERICH

WestBow Press books may be ordered through booksellers or by contacting:

WestBow Press
A Division of Thomas Nelson & Zondervan
1663 Liberty Drive
Bloomington, IN 47403
www.westbowpress.com
1 (866) 928-1240

ISBN: 978-1-5127-5940-2 (sc)
ISBN: 978-1-5127-5941-9 (e)

Library of Congress Control Number: 2016916595

Print information available on the last page.

WestBow Press rev. date: 10/14/2016

Luke 24:45 “Then he opened their minds so they could understand the Scriptures.”

An awakened spirit recognizes God’s voice; an awakened life responds.

Dedicated to the memory of Jeff and Cindy Edington
You were both taken far too early, but I will see you
when my work here on Earth has finished.

Thank you, Christine: for your valuable feedback.
Without your edits, this would not have been possible.

Thank you Beckah Shae (album "Rest"), Audrey
Assad, and Kari Jobe for your music.
It often played in the background as I wrote this.

Thank you to my wife Kerri and daughter Anabelle.
You allowed me to commit my time and our finances to this project.

CONTENTS

FOREWORD

MY JOURNEY

Thank you for taking a few extra minutes to read the story of my journey. I know it is tempting to skip over forwards and introductions, but I assure you that this story will help to frame my reasons behind writing this book.

The dream of being a pastor:

I was raised in a Christian home in Indiana. Our family was the type that was in the church *every time the doors were open*, as people like to say. My earliest memories include my mother as a backup singer during the worship times. I still remember myself kneeling down at a pew in Sunday school around the age of 6, saying the sinner's prayer. I don't remember what I said exactly, but I know I confessed Jesus Christ as Lord and asked Him to forgive me of my sins for the very first time.

I went to a Christian school or was home schooled for the majority of my education until I graduated high school. As an early teen, I went on a missions trip to El Salvador and sat next to our district youth director on the airplane. I actually told him I planned to take his job eventually. We both had a laugh but didn't really talk about what exactly that would mean. I received my baptism in the Holy Spirit around the age of 14, and I immediately knew that God was calling me to be a youth pastor. Soon after that, I learned to play drums and began playing at my church. Then, I became a youth leader. I was heavily involved with all youth events and was in Bible Quiz (a competition of Bible knowledge). I always went to all the youth retreats and camps.

A large part of my teenage life was spent trying to explain this calling to friends and family (many of whom did not understand or agree). There was never a "rebellious streak" or any doubt in my mind of what direction I wanted to go. Right after high school, I went to a Bible college in Lafayette, Indiana where I was encouraged to serve and minister to all kinds of people in all kinds of ways (not just from a pulpit on a stage). At my college graduation, I *knew* I was going to go out there and conquer the world through youth ministry!

Reality sets in:

I quickly realized how difficult it would be to make a living as a youth pastor. I could not find a full-time job because most churches couldn't afford a full-time wage unless I could also lead worship (which I was certainly not qualified for). I did find part-time work at a small church but quickly discovered that I was not as ready as I had hoped. I was excited about teaching youth and encouraging them to follow God, but I was not quite an adult myself yet, and I had a hard time understanding boundaries and church politics. The paycheck was definitely not enough to pay the bills, and I only lasted a couple of months there. I still felt called to youth ministry but found myself in a place of confusion and frustration.

I remember working at a clothing store, a sandwich shop,

and trying to sell cell phones (all at the same time). Sometimes I would stop and wonder where I was heading in life. I soon got married and found myself thinking long term in regards to financial responsibility. I needed a bigger paycheck to get a nicer apartment. I had to start thinking further down the road of being a father someday. I was suddenly thinking about medical benefits and retirement plans. I took a good job at a bank which had much more career potential, but I was scared of losing my focus. I soon started volunteering at my church's youth group, which was incredible, but it was not where I thought I would be at this stage in my life. I was very disappointed. I second-guessed every decision I had made. I felt that I had let myself down. Still, life moved on. My wife and I were happy and were carving out a decent little life. We had a baby, got a house, went on vacations, and made plans for the future. During this journey, I still applied for youth pastor job openings, but most of them could only pay part time or required me to move, or were just not the right fit. Working at a bank turned into a career doing loans and mortgages, then selling life insurance, and I just found myself lost in a career in which I honestly had no interest. That was tough, and I often questioned God about the direction my life was going…then, the direction changed.

A time to reinvent:

At a very young age, my daughter had a serious accident and had to be flown by helicopter to a hospital. This eventually led to severe financial stress. We had excellent credit and had paid off two cars but could not keep up with the medical bills and we had to file bankruptcy. My wife was originally from Ontario, and she had always wanted to go back. She was thinking about leaving her job, and I was ready for anything different. In just a couple of weeks, we both quit our jobs and moved to Belle River, Ontario. The plan was to stay with her parents for a while and just see where the journey would lead us. I hoped maybe this was my chance. I hoped I would be able to reinvent myself. I wanted to get back on the track of being a youth pastor.

At that time, I started being more dedicated to journaling and putting my notes together in a book format. (This encouraged me to start my blog becomingevermindful.wordpress.com and write this book.) I tried to get connected; I got to know a local pastor pretty quickly and even applied at a couple of churches there, but could not work in Ontario until I had my work permit. We were close enough to the border that I was able to commute. However, my license to sell life insurance was only good in Indiana. I figured I would just find a quick job to get us by until my work permit was approved, so I started to work at a pharmacy/convenience store. They told me when I was hired that I would soon be trained to be the manager (which was the only reason I took the job). That hiring manager left soon after I was brought on. The new manager did not like the idea of someone so new becoming a manager (which is understandable). He did soon put me in a supervisory role, and it was going well enough, but it was not the career I was hoping for. The weeks turned into months which turned into over two years waiting to get my work permit. I started getting that disappointed feeling again. I was going to church faithfully and just holding onto the hope that I would find myself in the ministry somehow. When I did get that work permit, I started looking more seriously at all my transferable skills. I had no real experience working at a church by now, and many churches simply could not take my resume seriously.

The big move:

My wife had been looking for jobs for me online while I was beating the pavement. I was still open to going back to Indiana and applied at some churches there. I even interviewed for a couple of positions, but nothing was opening up. My wife and I were looking at any options we could find. My wife has a cousin that lived in Calgary, Alberta with whom she was very close. They came up with a plan. We could start looking for jobs there (as there was a bit of an economic boom going on there) and I could live with her family until I got settled. Another store much like the one I was working for at that time was hiring. They were offering a management position which would include the salary we would require for me to get my own place soon. The catch was that my daughter had just started school (grade 3) so it would not be a good idea to move across the country since we didn't know if it would work out. Still, it was our best option. I wrote down God's words to Jacob from Genesis 28:15 that "I am with you and will watch over you wherever you go, and I will bring you back to this land. I will not leave you until I have done what I have promised you." I moved by myself in October of 2012, leaving my wife and young daughter behind, holding on to the hope that I would make enough money to move them out with me soon. After two months, I was starting to get a feeling of confidence. I was paid pretty well, and I was getting involved in a local church. I couldn't help but feel that I was starting to settle for a career outside of full-time ministry (remember my life's goal and plan was to be in full-time ministry) and it was eating me alive.

Bad news:

Unfortunately, I did not have to settle for that career because the company fired me after only two months citing that they were hiring another, more-experienced manager and I was no longer the best fit. WHAT?? What was this all supposed to mean? I had already paid for a round-trip plane ticket as I had planned to visit my family for Christmas. Now, I had to face them all and celebrate Christmas with that on my mind. On my way home from work that day, I called the only ministry connection I had made in Calgary (from the church I was attending). I didn't know him (Pastor Derek) that well and I was a crying, blubbering mess as I explained my situation. He recalled a pastor from a local church that had mentioned in passing that he was looking for a part-time youth pastor. Well, that was enough to restore my hope in God's plan. "Maybe this all happened for a reason," I said to myself. I called that pastor (Pastor John) and set up an interview for the first week of January when I planned to return. I went to Ontario and tried celebrating Christmas without worrying too much about all this (and only told my wife and a couple of others what was really going on). I had a great time with my wife and daughter and our families and nervously awaited the upcoming interview.

New year, new hope:

So I came back to Calgary, interviewed for the job, and was offered the position. Although it was only a part-time job, I saw it as a fantastic opportunity. There was not much pay, no health benefits, no retirement plan but it was something. I prayed that it would open the doors I needed to move my family to live with me. Shortly after accepting this position, another job literally fell into my lap. I wasn't looking for the job. The guy I was living with owned the company and the position had recently become vacant. It was a perfect fit as it still allowed me to work at the church. NOW, I HAD ARRIVED!!

Not quite so fast:

By now, I had been working at the church and the flooring company for six months. I had my own place, and I had just bought a car (as I had left our old one behind with my wife), so we made the final decision that this was the time for my wife and daughter to move. We still had some of our belongings in a storage unit in Indiana, so my wife and her brother rented a truck and drove down to get it all. We paid for the plane tickets and for the moving company to bring everything out. Everything was perfect. Seriously, I couldn't have scripted it much better. I had even already signed our daughter up for school and paid the fees. Then, the flooring company decided that I was not the best fit for the position and let me go! The same week that my wife moved (with a semi full of our stuff), I found myself with only a part-time, ministry position!

Still believing:

The next five months would be the hardest ones of my life. The flooring company allowed me to work a general labor job, but it was for far less pay. The board at the church knew my situation and allowed me to work a few extra hours, but it was barely enough to get by. I had many fights with God while I was grouting floors and caulking showers (which I still detest to this day). I literally threw fits and asked God how He could do this to me. Through regular phone calls to my mom, who had always been my rock and my prayer warrior, I knew God had not forgotten me…but it sure felt like it.

FINALLY:

Finally, I was offered a full-time position with a Christian organization that helps people who are experiencing homelessness. It was ministry. It was full-time. It was a solid career that about which I was excited. I did that job along with youth ministry and, for the first time in a long time, we were happy. We really felt peace. We loved our new life; my daughter made lots of new friends at her school, and I loved my job.

Still Being Tested:

The unfortunate part of my new career was that I was so far away from my family in Indiana. In October of 2014, my mother passed away. It was sudden and completely unexpected, and I was not able to visit her in the hospital. It was tough. I eventually had to resign from the church as it was very hard for me to do both in my mental state. In October of 2015, my step-father passed away. It was also sudden, and completely unexpected, and I was not even able to attend the funeral. I found myself questioning God on an entirely new level. Sometimes there are just no real answers.

In Conclusion:

I am still working as a chaplain at the organization helping the homeless, and I actually love my life now. I am glad we moved to Calgary, but I don't understand why we have to be so far from my family. However, when I pray about this, God confirms within my spirit that this is where He has called me to be. There are always twists and turns in life. No matter how well you plan things; there are often unexpected forks in the road. In my position, I often hear terrible stories from our guests. But many stories I hear are often quite amazing. Other people don't get to hear these stories because their fear of being close to the homeless prevents them from getting past their biases. I often tell my clients that what has helped me remain steady in times of turmoil has always been to simply trust in God's word which is really what this book is all about. I remember that Moses told the Israelites (in Deuteronomy 31:8), "The Lord himself goes before you and will be with you; he will never leave you nor forsake you. Do not be afraid; do not be discouraged." Life is a journey that we can never fully plan out or understand. Our job is to become mindful of what God is saying and what Jesus Christ has done and what the Holy Spirit is doing through each stride we take. Please enjoy your journey of Becoming Ever Mindful!

CHAPTER 1

WHAT IS BECOMING EVER MINDFUL?

TO BEGIN, I MUST first fully establish what being "ever mindful" means. Although the idea may seem obvious, this proposition will open the door to a thorough, meaningful soul search. So let's start at first glance, to be ever mindful is very straightforward and almost obvious, (and I laugh as I pause for five whole minutes to come up with the best words to define it):

> *Becoming Ever Mindful means focusing your mind and actions towards your number one goal at all times and not allowing any distractions to deter your course.*

Completely zero in, line up all your actions in accordance with your number one goal.

To possess this state of mind requires much hard work. You will have to learn to reexamine yourself regularly so that everything in your life lines up to get you wherever it is you want to be. Thus, the foundations of this idea can be applied to just about anything. Someone training to be an Olympic athlete must be ever mindful in the way they train and eat. The investment banker must be ever mindful of the financial market's performance and how it will affect their clients.

The purpose of this book, however, is much deeper, for it is my plan to explore how to become ever mindful of our Christian faith and what God wants for our lives. This way, not a day will pass where we go about our business without first asking for God's direction. So many of us have plans and things we hope to accomplish and have seen many years go by with no progression. The precise reason for this is because it is too easy for us to allow things, events or people to get in our way, slow us down, and ultimately hold us back. We often get sidetracked because we are not remaining mindful of our goals in every action.

You must realize that God is present and wants to speak to you at all times.

You will have to practice listening to His voice when a noisy crowd is all around you. *You will have to welcome God into every space of your life.* Unfortunately, it often takes some misfortune to make us desperate before we take action. In the same way that many drug addicts won't change until they are on the brink of losing everything, we seem only to act when we get to the point where we have nothing left to lose before we are willing to risk it all. I suggest that we learn from this behavior before it's too late before we let ten more years go by and look back in disbelief *before we completely miss out on what God wants for our lives.* I guess that's why I finally buckled down and finished this book. I knew this is what God wanted me to do and because of my previous situation, I had no real excuses anymore.

Allow God, His Word and His moral fiber to affect your every action, every word, and every thought.

The idea is to keep whatever it is that is most important to you in front of your mind and actions so that everything you do reflects and aligns itself with that goal. I firmly believe that some of you reading this book right now are at the point of desperation. *You may feel like you just can't do it anymore.* Life has not turned out the way you planned or dreamed, and you are not happy. Each day passes by, and you feel like you are slipping further away from your dreams. You've lost your joy and your feeling of purpose. That does not mean that everything in your life is a wreck. If you are like me when I felt that I would never find the right ministry position, you probably feel okay with your life, but know it's not the vibrant, exciting, enjoyable experience for which you had hoped. Maybe you're going to the same job every day and know that it's not what you want to do, but you're afraid of losing your security. Some of you may have friends in your life that are leading you down the wrong path and you know you should move on, but you don't want to be lonely. It is likely that *many of you just know there's something more out there,* and you just can't figure out what it is or how to attain it. I understand, because I have felt some of those feelings myself and these ideas that I am about to share are what helped me get out of that funk.

The one thing you can control is your thought process.

You can become more mindful of whatever it is God is putting in your heart and you can start making changes accordingly. Romans 12:2 sums it up perfectly, "Do not conform to the pattern of this world, but be transformed by the renewing of your mind. Then you will be able to test and approve what God's will is—his good, pleasing and perfect will." On this journey of becoming ever mindful, you will learn to be on fire for God and not lukewarm or cold. We can no longer be nonchalant about our faith walk! I believe it is as easy as (1) learning never to give up on your dreams and, (2) remembering God's promises at all times.

How can you keep your faith and thoughts in line when it seems like everything around you is falling apart? How will you have the strength to keep fighting when you see no light at the end of the tunnel and you have lost your hope? The answer is only in getting passionate about your dreams and having the discipline to carry out that passion in every decision you make. I will explore a deeper understanding of God's vision for your life and the necessary discipline later in the book.

You will see your actions change as you line yourself up with the promises of God's Word.

You will learn to continue the course because you believe in something greater. The ever- mindful person has a goal but is ok when plans change. He or she understands that someone else may have a better idea and will be willing to take advice. And the ever-mindful person will become more flexible and does not get offended when God changes his or her direction.

What has made this idea of being ever mindful tug at me for the past few years is the fact that it is such a simple concept in theory but tough to live out. Even though it is something I believe in and am passionate about, I still struggle with it. The reason I'm writing this book is that *I believe this idea has the power to enable a Christian to not only survive, but soar!*

I recently read the autobiography of Drew Brees, easily my favorite quarterback in the NFL. He talks about how a quarterback has to be ready to change his whole plan in a split second. Even a backup quarterback who may not play very much still must know all the plays perfectly. He must have on his uniform. And he must be on the sidelines ready to play at a moment's notice. In this same way, a Christian should be engaged and ready to be used by God at a moment's notice.

Don't worry, though; not everything has to change all at once. I've played drums for the better part of my life now, and I know that after banging those drum heads so many times they get out of tune, and it takes some work to get them back into shape. If I check them regularly, it is not too difficult to tune them. But if I wait too long, then they will warp and be much harder to fix.

You will need to allow God to work on you gradually and often.

Allow His word to slowly permeate your whole being like how a roast in the oven slowly absorbs all the other flavors surrounding it. I believe that's what Joshua meant when he said in his book (chapter1, verse 8), "Keep this Book of the Law always on your lips; meditate on it day and night, so that you may be careful to do everything written in it. Then you will be prosperous and successful." Apparently, from that scripture, there is a specific order in the design of how God wants us to walk with Him. Becoming ever mindful of God's plan for your life starts with an understanding of His Word. John 1:1 says "In the beginning was the Word, and the Word was with God, and the Word was God." You must know the Word to know God. I believe God wants to direct each step of our lives. In Psalm 119:105 the author said, "Your word is a lamp for my feet, a light for my path." The scripture would imply that we are in the dark without His light to lead us. This anonymous author understood that we are completely lost if we do not hold dear to those most sacred words of God's divine law.

Have you ever tried to walk through a room in complete darkness? Understanding these principles does not mean we have to be doing God's work every second of our day, but it does mean that we need to stay in tune spiritually and we need to be prepared to do the work. So from that standpoint, it is implied that we should be memorizing scripture as to be prepared. Philippians 4:8 says "Finally, brothers and sisters, whatever is true, whatever is noble, whatever is right, whatever is pure, whatever is lovely, whatever is admirable—if anything is excellent or praiseworthy—*think about such things*." (Emphasis added.) We do not pretend the bad things don't exist, but we will make a decision to focus our attention so that we continue in our true north direction.

You must have a regular devotion time with God.

It is not my place to tell you exactly how, but I will say that devotion time must be an important part of your journey so that you do keep your mind focused on the good things. It is critical that we give the Lord the opportunity to work on us regularly. When is the last time you truly meditated on God's Word? I know we're busy and that it's hard to fit God in sometimes. I have heard people suggest that we should count God as a scheduled appointment, such as making time early in the morning before the kids wake up or every night before you go to bed. Spending time with God should be your own personal time. Let it be as simple as reading a short devotional or as in-depth as having a long study of the Bible, but make it a habit. Also note that when you do anything for too long, it is very easy to get trapped in the habit of doing it just to do it so make sure you change it up sometimes.

For me, I like to have no distractions around me. I like to

go to our basement and put on some worship mus
God's presence for a while. I keep a notebook clo
carnal (worldly, sinful nature) brain will remind
things I should be doing instead of "just sitting there in the dark." This way I can write it down and deal with it later. Then I can also write down anything that the Holy Spirit impresses upon me. I always try to get my mind focused on God and only God. Sometimes I just sit there and sing my own songs of worship. I don't mean to tell you how to pray; I just want to encourage you to be intentional about it. I love the saying that *prayer doesn't change God, it changes us*. That is what happens when you train yourself to be ever mindful of God's agenda. You will become nicer to people, you will understand your situation better, your thoughts and words will be kinder.

Becoming ever mindful is not synonymous with becoming perfect.

Through this journey, you will learn to depend on God more fully. You will learn to respond to that tug in your spirit more quickly. You will recognize His guidance in a noisy crowd. You will begin to feel that gentle nudge of guidance even in seemingly trivial decisions. I know this because it is all based on God's word and His promises to us. I will share some stories where this has happened to me that I still cannot explain. Please understand that you will always make mistakes but God can only work with someone who is brave enough to make those mistakes as you will find in countless events told in the Bible. Hopefully, those mistakes will become less frequent and less potent.

In becoming ever mindful, you will find yourself staying the course more readily. When you do fail, you will get back in line more quickly. With this said, let us learn to continually pray for

God's direction even with the "small things." We cannot blame God for the outcome of something if we did not ask for His guidance in the first place. I can't tell you how many times that I've just acted on my own in a situation without realizing that I never stopped to ask God what He wanted me to do. I have a bad habit of asking for forgiveness later instead of permission before. Why do so easily allow my thoughts to go unchecked?

We must learn to guard ourselves against walking aimlessly.

I pray that, through the journey of this book, you become more aware of your thoughts, become more intentional with your words, and become disciplined with the path you take in life. Becoming ever mindful works like a sound investment. It must be rebalanced based on dips and surges in the market. You can't leave it on aggressive or safe investing all the time. Your walk with God must also be rebalanced. Where have you veered off track? Can you even see the track anymore? God will not force you back onto the track. It must be your decision. Revelation 3:20 records Jesus saying, "Here I am! I stand at the door and knock. If anyone hears my voice and opens the door, I will come in and eat with that person, and they with me."

Practice Point: Stop for a few moments and think about what it is that you consider your primary goal. What are your core values? What is the one thing that you hope is said of you when you are not in the room? It may be best to write these things down and pray about them as you continue reading.

CHAPTER 2

WHAT DO YOU BELIEVE?

BEFORE WE DIG TOO deep here, there are a couple of things we must explore. The ever mindful concept is one of those "easy to figure out, hard to master" kind of things. I think what makes this most difficult to apply in our daily Christian walk is that the majority of us differ drastically in our view of what a "good Christian" looks like. For instance, some more orthodox or traditional believers may say you should not ever cut your hair or drink any alcohol. The strictest Roman Catholic will never have sexual relations with their spouse unless they are trying to have a baby, but many are ok with drinking alcohol every once in a while. I was raised in a house that was very free-spirited but extremely devoted to church and God, and we never had alcohol in the house. I'm not trying to make a case for or against alcohol, but the "gray areas" of our faith can be hard to identify and even harder to clarify. What is most intriguing to me is that no matter what your core beliefs were at one time, you can and usually do change them as you go through life. In extreme cases, I've heard of very solid Christians becoming murderers or alcoholics or child abusers or just walking away from their faith altogether. How many pastors have completely fallen away and turned their back on God's work or had a lapse in character that was detrimental to the very message they were trying to relay? Does that lapse in character mean he or she is no longer a child of God? What's fascinating is that on the flip side of the coin, I'm sure we all know a few people who would never dare profess to be a Christian in that term but are very kind and selfless and giving. (I know many "non-Christians that are kinder than many who claim to be Christians.) Most of us can quote some scriptures or recite some poem or song we learned in Sunday school. Many of these activities lead to learned behaviors.

Ask yourself this: if you had not been raised the way you were or had some of your life experiences, would you still believe the way you do?

We become who we are based on the situations in which we are brought up. A lot of times we aren't ever forced to examine our beliefs. If you read my forward ("My Journey"), you'll already know that the first 20 years of my life were spent in the "church bubble." I was almost oblivious to the rest of the world around me. My mom was very active in church and made sure our family was in there any time the doors were opened. Being Christian was honestly a way of life for me. I was quite confident in my relationship with God. It was very deep and personal but I never really had to examine why I believed. It was just who I was and, honestly, I loved it. I never got tired of that lifestyle,

I went back to a public school for my senior year (Grade 12 for the Canadians), so I could graduate with my friends. By that time, being Christian was such a lifestyle that I didn't have much in common with many of the other teenagers. Church was still the primary focus of my free time, so the question of what I deeply believed was one I never had to explore. By that time, even the "big things" like partying and drinking and drugs and sex were no real temptation to me mostly because I was unaware. I knew those things were out there, but I also felt they were wrong, so I simply didn't do them. I certainly was not perfect (and still am not, of course), I was just a little different than the typical, un-churched teen. *I didn't mind being different from my peers and I am proud that I did remain true to my beliefs.* In Bible college, we were involved in ministry from day one. We were going to the dark places, taking God's love to places where most people had no hope and no cares.

I have had the good fortune to travel all around the U.S. and even other countries to see all types of ministry. I actually, physically saw lines of kids excited because they were going to get a bowl of white rice. We handed out 10 cent candies and trinkets and the kids flocked to us like it was Christmas morning. I was even with a ministry group that was detained and police escorted out of Morocco for handing out Bibles. Still, I never had to question why I believed what I believed.

When I first stepped out of my bubble and the people around me weren't all Christians, I struggled for a while. The others didn't necessarily understand *or care to understand* how God wanted to work in their lives. Now I was living among the non-Christians more than the Christians, and that's where my journey really began. When I invited people to church and they said no, I still had to see them the next day. I had to try to comprehend why the church was not exciting to them the way it was to me. They sometimes had convincing arguments about how they thought God was not there for them when they needed Him. Some felt that there was no Jesus, so it did not matter how they lived. Others would ask me very real and honest questions about why I believe so firmly.

For the first time in my life, I was forced to ask myself that question. What do I believe?

It seems like such a simple question at first, but if you stop and think about it, it's like a small battle. What do I believe? The question is not, "what did my parents teach me," and not, "what is the best sermon I heard," or, "what are some of my favorite Bible passages," but "what are *my* real foundational beliefs?" I started to ask myself these questions. Is there really a heaven? Did God actually create everything? Does He control everything in my life or merely help me along the way or maybe He just expects me to figure it out and He will tell me how I did at the end? I thought I knew all that perfectly but when I worked with someone eight hours a day, five days a week that blatantly disagreed, I began to run out of arguments. I was never forced to have those conversations before. My new friends would bring up things that I didn't understand and point out facts and questions that rocked the foundations of my arguments. Then I would wonder. Am I right? How do I know I'm right? *Do I doubt God because I question things I don't understand?* Where is the line between the absolute truths that I believe whole-heartedly and things I agree with but am not entirely dogmatic towards?

I guess there's no single or simplistic answer to a lot of those questions, but I have learned a lot through examining myself and praying about my beliefs. I have made it a habit of studying the history of the Bible and beliefs for myself. I understand now that becoming ever mindful about what I believe is a journey where God reveals himself to me a little more each day. But I have to search for Him. The sons of Korah who devoted themselves to worship said in Psalms 42:7 that "the deep calls to the deep." What that means to me is that when you learn to have that close, intimate relationship with God, His Spirit enriches you from inside so that it's more than knowledge, God becomes part of your soul. That's all well and good, but it still doesn't give us concrete answers to all our questions which kind of concerns me. Honestly, I think that's the point. You may be in the same place I was (and still am at times) and feel like you'll never have the right words to say but trust me when I say this:

God will reveal Himself when He needs to, not when we need Him to.

Hebrews 4:12 says "For the word of God is alive and active. Sharper than any double-edged sword, it penetrates even to dividing soul and spirit, joints and marrow; it judges the thoughts and attitudes of the heart." In my opinion, this means that the Word will reveal to you what you need if you dig deep into it. I think it is important to remember the next verse which says that nothing is hidden from His sight. God sees and knows our heart, mind, and emotions. I believe He wants to minister to you in all those areas through His Word. It's kind of like those iridescent neckties that look like one color until the light hits it differently. When Paul was trying to battle the deception of Gnosticism, he told the believers in Colosse that the wisdom and knowledge of the mystery of God are hidden in Christ (see Colossians 2). James 1:5 says, "If any of you lacks wisdom, you should ask God, who gives generously to all without finding fault, and it will be given to you." We must learn to trust God and allow Him to give us wisdom but also recognize when to leave the rest to Him.

I think this is a great spot to establish some of my absolute truths. I do believe God is the omnipotent creator of everything, the first and the last. I do believe our Heavenly Father wanted us to have perfect communion with Him, but He did not want to force it upon us, so He gave us a choice. The choice to follow our desires instead of His perfect plan resulted in sin and complete separation from our loving Father. There is a place of complete separation from God called hell and it will be a place of torment for the people who willfully pushed God's love and grace out of their lives. Romans 6:23 states plainly "For the wages of sin is death!" *The only way back to Him was through a blood sacrifice.* This was a sacrifice which, in the Old Testament times, meant literally transferring your sins onto the scapegoat (that's where the term comes from). I am glad that, in His love, God sent His Son Jesus to live a perfect life and die for us and rise again to establish a new covenant between God and us.

Because Jesus went through the crucifixion, we no longer have to do things under that old covenant. This son had to be brutally punished and hung in pain and agony which words cannot express so that the door could be re-opened and forgiveness could be given. Romans 3:24 says "and all are justified freely by his grace through the redemption that came by Christ Jesus." I believe that son was resurrected from the dead to defeat the power of death. I believe that Jesus ascended into heaven so that the Holy Spirit could reside with us. It is the Holy Spirit who is presently speaking to us as our advocate, helper, counselor, comforter (the Greek word is paraclete). He will continually communicate with our spirit which God created in us to help us remain in line with God's plan.

Finally, I believe the Bible is God's written Word, and no one will convince me otherwise.

The Bible was written over a span of more than 1500 years. It has more than 40 authors all with different backgrounds and lifestyles yet they told one single story of a creator that desperately wanted

His people to love and follow Him because His way led to peace and joy. I believe the Bible's validity is proven in many historical, archeological, and scientific ways. Check out Probe Ministries for an exhaustive list of facts that back up the Bible (https://www.probe.org/ancient-evidence-for-jesus-from-non-christian-sources-2/). Also see "scienceandfaith.com" and John Lennox's "God's Undertaker: Has Science Buried God?" There were more than 350 Old Testament predictions fulfilled in Christ's life. It is not just a book! The Holy Bible is not just a story! Jesus was not just a man! Second Timothy 3:16 "All Scripture is God-breathed." In my opinion, this case is closed! History and science prove the validity of the Bible and many of its events. One day I will be in heaven and will reunite with my creator and my loved ones that have passed away; as such, I will not fear death.

My job here, however, is not to make you believe what I believe.

Acts 17:11 records "Now the Berean Jews were of more noble character than those in Thessalonica, for they received the message with great eagerness and examined the Scriptures every day to see if what Paul said was true." I pray you do the same. I only tell you what I believe to set a basis, but you should examine this for yourself as well. *What I feel God wants me to bring attention to here is that each of us needs to get in his or her special prayer place and explore these questions.* What do you believe? Why do you believe it? Are there questions you have where you have not sought answers? It's ok to wonder about your core beliefs as long as it leads to a desire to educate yourself further. What is a "good Christian?" What allows a person access to heaven? What can send that same individual to hell? Ask yourself these questions and others you think of, do the research and personal soul search. Write down your answers. Pray about them so you have an answer for that co-worker who asks why you go to church.

This is not a new idea. When Paul was teaching young Timothy, he said the Holy Scripture would make him wise. Equip yourself so you are prepared if you have to debate God's existence and His word. Those times should not cause you to lose yourself or your faith in a heated argument. (I rarely experience these discussions going that far.) Opposition creates an opportunity to share your personal experience. I'm just suggesting that you attempt to know what you believe. I may not have all the answers, but I know what I believe and am confident about who I am in Christ.

Practice Point: I will end this chapter with a challenge. Is being a Christian just something that you know or is it something you are. Seek God to find out why you believe what you believe and write those things down so that in your dark times when life has thoroughly beaten you down, you can go back to those words to remind yourself why you began this fight in the first place.

What are my core values as a Christian?

Where do I struggle as a Christian? i.e. judgement

CHAPTER 3

HOW GOD SEES YOU

I WANT TO ASK a question, and I want you to pause and think about it for a moment before you read any further. It's a very simple question, but you will soon see how your response can limit you or free you. The question is; who are you? Don't rush the answer. What's the first thing that comes to mind? I know it's tempting to read ahead but just trust me here. Who are you? Get past the superficial surface answers. I'm sure you know I'm setting you up for something but just humor me and think deeper. Throughout this book, we will discover some people from the Bible and from more modern history who either did not know how to answer that question, forgot the answer to that question, or who were confident in their answer and lived to prove it.

My plan for this chapter is that we all learn to see ourselves the way God sees us.

I will warn you that it is difficult but only because you are probably your own worst enemy and will likely get in your own way many times. Attempting to answer that question honestly will begin a deep soul search and probably come to fruition only through many tears and prayers. *Let us first establish who you are not.* Your name is not who you are. Your job or schooling is not who you are. Who you are is not defined by your abilities or disabilities. It is not your shortcomings or even your victories. Who you are is not merely the image you see in the mirror or wish you saw in the mirror. It is not the failures of your past or the present situation that seems to put limitations on you. Who you are is who God created you to be! God sees more in you than you can ever possibly see in yourself. Read the following statements out loud over yourself.

YOU ARE NOT what people say you are.
YOU ARE NOT weak.
YOU ARE NOT disgusting.
YOU ARE NOT incapable.
YOU ARE NOT defeated.

You may have shortcomings, and maybe you lash out at someone or harbor unforgiveness at times, but don't let those things define you. That's your carnal, worldly flesh, not you. That's who you become when you forget to renew your mind daily and when you are not operating in the fruit of the spirit.

So, who are you?

Who you are can be simplified by two consecutive verses in the Bible. Romans 8:16+17 "The Spirit himself testifies with our spirit that we are God's children. Now if we are children, then we are heirs—heirs of God and co-heirs with Christ, if indeed we share in his sufferings in order that we may also share in his glory." Please pause and read that again. Say it out loud until you believe it with every fiber of your being. You will never be able to change what you consider your identity until you grasp those scriptures wholly. I'm not sure about you, but I want to share in His glory. I want to share in Jesus Christ's exaltation, achievement, splendor, beauty, and overcoming joy. The truth of it though is that we usually are not sharing that glory. Not because we aren't trying hard enough but because we are not believing hard enough. We get too caught up in the things we can't change, the things that are none of our business, or the things that we have no control over.

In my profession, I notice people who are suffering from things they did not do to themselves but were done to them. People, this idea of becoming ever mindful is powerful because when we completely surrender everything to God and make a conscious effort to walk in His love we become who we were meant to be. The Bible tells us in Ephesians 1:4+5 "For he chose us in him before the creation of the world to be holy and blameless in his sight. In love he predestined us for adoption to sonship through Jesus Christ, in accordance with his pleasure and will." That means before you were formed in the womb, God knew you and had a plan and hope for you. Your thought life is the only thing that can get in your way. He promised to walk with you every step of the way because God has an invested interest in your success!

I believe what Proverbs says in 18:21 "The tongue has the power of life and death, and those who love it will eat its fruit." so let's speak some life into your spirit right now.

Stop for a moment and claim these things over your life. (Have some tissue ready, I still tear up when I read this to myself.)

I am not dead *in transgression. I am alive in Christ! (1 Cor 15:22)*

I am not afraid. *God is with me. He will strengthen me and help me. (Isaiah 41:10)*

I can do all things *through my Lord who gives me the strength! (Philippians 4:10)*

Nothing shall be impossible *with God on my side. (Luke 1:37)*

The Spirit of the sovereign Lord is on *me because the Lord has anointed me. (Isaiah 61:1)*

I know that in all things God works for the good *of those who love Him, who have been called according to His purpose. (Romans 8:28)*

I am not terrified, *the Lord, who is among us, is a great and awesome God! (Deut 7:21)*

My hope is in the Lord *and He will renew my strength. I will soar on wings like eagles; I will run and not grow weary, I will walk and not be faint. (Isaiah 40:31)*

I consider that our present sufferings are not worth comparing *with the glory that will be revealed in us. (Romans 8:18)*

I am anointed! I am chosen by God! I am called to overcome! God approves of me and loves me! I AM GOD'S CHILD!

The proposition of understanding our identity brings me to the first person in the Bible that I want to explore a little deeper. Although the scriptures do not expand on his story very much, we can learn a lot from the information we do have. His name is Mephibosheth. His is a story about losing touch with his identity. Unfortunately, it ruined most of his life. I had never noticed this

name in the Bible until I was reading about him in a book by T.D. Jakes years ago and it has stuck with me ever since. His story was recorded in Second Samuel.

Mephibosheth was Jonathan's son, King Saul's grandson. That means he had royal blood flowing through his veins. When Mephibosheth was just five years old, both King Saul and Jonathan were killed in battle with the Philistines. His nurse heard of the tragedy and picked him up to rush away, but Mephibosheth fell and became crippled in both feet. We don't hear anything else from him until years later when King David searches for someone from Saul's house to whom he can show kindness.

The people Mephibosheth loved and trusted the most let him down.

I'm sure his will and his heart were broken just as badly as his legs because it seems to have messed him up for the rest of his life. He forgot who he was and failed to see himself the way God saw him. I don't know exactly how many years passed between the unfortunate accident and the time David found him. When he was found, he was living in a land called Lo Debar which means "cut off from communication." He basically became an unknown with no future and no hope. I'm sure it was devastating watching David become king instead of someone such as himself who was a true heir to the throne. It is very likely that he was in a place where no one was around to build him up or remind him of what God could do through his life. Fortunately, God still used King David to restore Mephibosheth. Perhaps the saddest part of the story is that when Mephibosheth was brought forward to be blessed, his reply to King David was "What is your servant, that you should notice a dead dog like me? (2 Samuel 9:8)" Wow, you talk about low self-esteem! His perception of himself was as little as it could be. Dogs were generally considered dirty, disgusting, ravagers in that time. How sad it must have been for David to hear that. He would have known that this man had royal blood in his veins. Mephibosheth was the son of one of David's dearest friends, Jonathan who helped him flee the wrath of Saul.

Has something happened in your past that you are allowing to hold you back?

Paul said to in Hebrews 12:1 "Therefore, since we are surrounded by such a great cloud of witnesses, let us throw off everything that hinders and the sin that so easily entangles. And let us run with perseverance the race marked out for us." Sin is not always our most severe hindrance. The pain in your past can be more detrimental to your success than you may realize. A bad habit or a sour attitude is often a symptom of a hurt you have not released. You will never become ever mindful of your number one goal if you continue holding on to your pain. I'm not a therapist or a psychologist by any means, but I hear about these hangups from my clients very often. Many of them are lost in life because they cannot let go of the past. They can no longer focus on their primary goal in life because they are distracted by the hurt. Being homeless is often a symptom of a long, difficult history.

I learned about the power of my past for myself by reading "Battlefield of the Mind" by Joyce Meyer. She reminds us that Satan already has the upper hand if we are beating ourselves down because of bad decisions or circumstances. You must learn to let go and begin the healing process by inviting the Holy Spirit to minister to that part of your life. It is painful. It's like cleaning out the closet of a spare bedroom where you just keep throwing stuff. You sometimes have to take it all out and reexamine why you're keeping those things. If you don't need it, or it is just wasting space, you must throw it out and put the space to better use. You can do this with your spiritual life as well.

Throw off the hurt and allow God to fill that part of your mind with His love so He can use you the way he wants.

Even for me, it is easy to write this down but hard to live. I know from my own experience and my struggles with confidence that it is tough for me to accept love and live a life unrestrained by my personal shortcomings and doubts. Knowing our identity is another area where it is imperative that we learn to become ever mindful of the way God sees us. Let's think about another story from the Bible. Moses came from a very difficult upbringing, to say the least. Having a mother that let you float down a river and just land wherever could have caused some confusion with his identity (although, we know it was for a good reason). Much later in his life, when God called Moses, God knew something about Moses that he did not understand yet.

God appointed Moses to free the Egyptian slaves and lead them to the Promised Land, but it didn't make any sense to Moses. From a logical mindset, there's no way God should use him. The last time he was seen with the Egyptians, he lost his temper and killed someone and ran away! Now God is telling him to go back there! Read Exodus chapter 4 and pay attention to all the various reasons Moses came up with as to why the people would not listen to him. What I love is that every question Moses could conjure up brought forth the same type of answer. God said, "I will be with you." I can picture a little smirk on God's face as He shook his head. *Moses did not yet appreciate the fact that God's ways are higher than his own, and that was all that would matter.*

We can't blame Moses for feeling a little intimidated and alone at times. I know I have pondered those same things over the years when things didn't seem to be going my way. I've caught myself throwing my hands up and exclaiming, "I just don't have any luck." We must be careful that these fits do not change our perception of our identity in Christ.

I want to share a couple of things here that remind me of how God cares for me. They're simple, but that's why I like them. One day I was at work showing some pictures of my daughter to a co-worker, and a customer saw them. She started talking about how beautiful my daughter Anabelle is and said she wanted to buy her something. I was grateful and anticipated a little trinket or maybe a cheap doll or something but the next day that lady brought a bag from a major department store with a brand new winter coat! It had a matching scarf and hat too! Another time a different person heard me sneeze at work and ran out to her car and brought in a box of allergy medicine and nose spray. What are the chances that she would have that in her car and be willing to give them to a stranger? These aren't anything earth shattering, but they remind me that God can use anyone at any time. Why can't that be God working through others to bless me? It's hard for me to believe that someone is that interested in my well-being, but I KNOW God is!

We have to learn to allow ourselves to be loved by God.

I remember a time that a lady wanted to buy me a Pepsi because I told her she was my last customer of the day. Looking back, I realize now that she wanted to buy it for me as a little night cap. I declined but talked to my wife Kerri about it the next day, and she told me that I should have let the customer buy it. She reminded me that God could have been using that lady to bless me. *Why are we so afraid to allow someone to go out of their way for us?* Why do I feel undeserving when an individual wants to bless me? It gives me joy and satisfaction to adorn someone else so why would I rob a stranger of their blessing by turning them down when they offer? You see, God doesn't have to move a mountain for you every time He wants to get your attention. He will make himself known in the little things if you open your eyes to see them. I want you to look back at the past few months of your life and think of stories like these that you have that no one else would care about but are dear to your heart. Once again, I think it best if you write them down and thank God for them to give your spirit a little pep talk. God is there in the shadows because He's the one who made the light which creates the shadows. So remember that God is on your side.

Who you are is how God sees you and not how you see yourself.

I will finish this chapter with a quick story about a lady who learned to see herself the way God sees her. Her name is Joni Eareckson Tada. She's very famous actually and has done numerous talk shows including Larry King Live. I encourage you to check out her website http://www.joniandfriends.org/about-us/history or her autobiography, "Joni: An Unforgettable Story." Please see one of those for the official story but I will give a brief overview now. It goes something like this: At age 17, she was getting ready to go to college and went for one last swim with her sister. Her sister dove first and began to swim. Joni dove soon after but hit her head on the ground which broke her neck and instantly paralyzed her. She lay limp in the water not able to even flail her arms to get her sister's attention. Her sister didn't know about it and started to swim away, but a crab pinched her toe causing her to turn around. Only because of that, she saw Joni laying there and swam over to pull her ashore.

In an instant, Joni's future hopes and plans were shattered. She lay in the hospital bed not able to move at all. She was fed through a tube and heard the devastating news that she would never walk again. Joni said that many friends and family visited her often, but she still had many lonely hours to lie there and think about her life. She became very depressed and tried to kill herself but could not move enough to finish it off. Her story includes asking her friends to help her end her life! Fortunately, one friend, in particular, Steve, did the opposite. He reminded her of God's love and His divine will. My favorite part of Joni's retelling of this conversation is the reminder of the abuse of Romans 8:28. Often, this verse is used with the intention that all things *ARE GOOD* with God. It does not say that! It says "All things *WORK FOR THE GOOD* (NIV)."

Joni, fortunately, came to the realization that God still had a plan for her. Finally, she prayed, "God if you're not going to let me die, then show me how to live." God answered that prayer. She has gone on to write many encouraging books, has set up a foundation to help those embracing a disability, and has even learned how to hold a paintbrush in her mouth to create some amazing paintings! You can view this on www.Youtube.com (search Joni Eareckson Tada on Art). *Joni's life is the epitome of an ever mindful life.* Joni learned to see herself the way God sees her. He doesn't see the shortcomings; He sees the potential. That's why Paul was able to say "That is why, for Christ's sake, I delight in weaknesses, in insults, in hardships, in persecutions, in difficulties. For when I am weak, then I am strong. (2 Corinthians 12:10)"

Practice Point: I could quote hundreds of scriptures here to tell you how God sees you, but I don't want to form your identity for you. You need to search your Bible for scriptures that jump out at you and write them down somewhere. (Or even use the ones I put in this chapter.) Pin them up in your visor in the car. Tape them to the mirror in your bathroom. Look at them every day until they permeate every thought you have and begin to impact what you think in regards to who you are.

CHAPTER 4

GOD CAN!

IMAGINE YOU HAVE A secret red phone in your basement. No one knows about it, and it's only for you to use. Imagine this phone goes straight to a multi-billionaire and anytime you need anything at all you just pick up the phone, and it rings to that person. No matter where this person is and no matter what he or she is doing, they pick up up and ask you what you need. Whatever the financial cost, it's yours because that person is your friend and wants to help you.

You have something better than that in your Heavenly Father!

Best of all, God is not there only for financial purposes! Prayer is your red phone that goes straight to God at a moment's notice. You just have to pick it up and believe that it will be done in His timing. God knows the answer before the question is asked. Please note that I am not a proponent for all "name it and claim it" theology. Much of that teaching is taken out of context and can easily lead you down the wrong path. However, according to the Psalmist David (in Psalms 56:8), God records our tears. Another poetic way to think of it, as in Flyleaf's song "Sorrow," is that "He knew each tear before it came." Do we fully comprehend what God can do? If Jesus could calm the winds and rains, then He can certainly calm the storms of your life. It is our responsibility to let Him take control.

Unfortunately, we are often like the disciples. The feeding of the 5000 is a well-known miracle recorded in the Gospels. Have you ever noticed that, only a short time later, the disciples were questioning how Jesus would feed 4000? The thing that is even more disappointing is that shortly after that, the disciples forget to bring enough bread for a journey they were going on and they got really anxious. Jesus had to remind them of what just happened only days before! Mark 8:17 says, "Aware of their discussion, Jesus asked them: 'Why are you talking about having no bread? Do you still not see or understand? Are your hearts hardened?'"

Becoming ever mindful equals becoming good at recognizing what battles are yours and what battles are God's. (Here's a hint: most of them are God's.) Jahaziel reminded his people in 2 Chronicles 20:15 "...Do not be afraid or discouraged because of this vast army. For the battle is not yours, but God's." *God is interested in your well-being.* We are His children, and He wants us to be happy. I believe that, in the midst of pain and tribulation, God is just chomping at the bit for us to recognize Him and fully depend on Him. Sometimes we just have to get out of the way and let Him do what He does. I believe that's what Jesus meant when He said His yoke is easy, and His burden is light in Matthew 11:30. The Bible says God knows how to give good gifts to His children even more than we do. I love my family more than I can describe with words. I want them to be happy. Nothing in the world will equal the joy I get when my daughter laughs. And nothing will equal the pain I feel when something hurts my wife's feelings. AND I LOVE TO GIVE THEM GIFTS! If I feel that way in my imperfect love, how much more amplified is that feeling in God's heart when He can give us gifts?

God does not like it when you are unhappy, and He can fix it!

There is a Christian musician named Tye Tribbett who I've been listening to a lot over the past few years. On his album Fresh, he has a song called, "When the Rocks Hit the Ground." It's a beautiful retelling of the story in John 8 where Jesus forgave the adulterous woman, and it got me thinking about the story a little deeper. Allow yourself to imagine being in her shoes for just a few minutes. Pretend you have just been caught doing something you know is wrong. You know you are living a life of sin and very likely do not want that lifestyle but see no way out. You knew the risks of where this out-of-control lifestyle would lead but just couldn't help yourself. Someone caught you doing the act you're so ashamed of and, now you are presented before a group of your neighbors as a guilty party in a judicial hearing. They stand ready to condemn you, and there is no question of your guilt. The laws are simple, and your sin merits death by stoning. Ashamed and afraid, you can't believe your life is going to end this way. The angry mob strong-arms you and drags you around like a lamb on its way to being sacrificed.

They stand you up before this man called Jesus the Christ that everyone has been talking about. He will become your haphazard, stand-in judge. You have no defense attorney arguing your case or trying to find a loophole to get you out of this mess and it wouldn't matter as you have no case to argue. What will this newfound judge say? You stand amidst the arguing and yelling and spitting. The people are scouring for more stones. Now, each member of the jury has a rock or flank of wood with arms cocked back ready to unleash. There is no one who would fault them for it either. These people are angry and spiteful and seem to be excited about bringing this judgment upon you. You close your eyes and wince in utter despair expecting that first stone to be thrown which will announce your final judgment. *Then you hear one sentence that instantly silences everything like a mute switch.* "If any of you is without sin, let him be the first to throw a stone at her. (John 8:7)"

Everyone is silent and for a few seconds you are in awe yourself. What does that mean? Why is this man not joining the angry crowd? The silence is broken by feet scuffling away; you hear gasps of disappointment and people whispering here and there. The most glorious sound you've ever imagined cuts the confusion in your mind as one stone causes a thud when it hits the dirt below. You are not entirely sure what the sound was. Maybe it was just your imagination. Maybe you're dreaming. Then the echo of ten more stones falling brings hope that it was not your imagination at all. Now it sounds like rain on a roof as the rest of the stones fall and everyone scurries off. You open your eyes to see that there is no more crowd, and you are standing beside this man, *just the two of you.* You try to hold it back, but a smile forces its way across your lips and tears flow like a waterfall. You know now that, for whatever reason, you are free! Somehow this Jesus found some angle that brought mercy from this wretched throng of new enemies.

You know you are undeserving of forgiveness and wonder why He would do this for a pathetic person such as yourself. "Who has condemned you?" He asks. Sobbing, your throat hurts as you try to reply, "No one, sir." "Then neither do I condemn you," Jesus declared. "Go now and leave your life of sin" (as recorded in John 8:11). A picture comes to my mind of Jesus picking her up and wrapping His arm around her, leading her to the well to get some fresh water. Maybe the two laugh as they sit and chat. He teaches her how to leave this life of shame behind. He counsels her to heal the wounds of her past that have led her down this road. Imagine the freedom and relief she must have felt. Folks, this story is real. More importantly, these same stories happen every day when a lost soul finds that there is freedom through Jesus Christ.

Your freedom begins when you see yourself the way God sees you and not the way society sees you.

Grasp on to the realization that God can turn a worthless life into a worthwhile one. I will never forget a time where God put someone in my life only to encourage me for a moment. I had written in my journal that morning, *"It feels like we're just drifting like we're not in control of anything. That would be okay if I could be assured that God is in control but I'm starting to wonder."* That night at work God reminded me that He *IS* listening and He *IS* in control. A customer walked up to me only to say that God saw how hard I was working and had not forgotten me. The customer finished with, "I want to tell you that great things are coming." Then the customer politely said he wasn't sure if that meant anything but he felt like he was supposed to tell me that. I smiled back at him and explained briefly about this book which I was trying to write and that I needed to hear that. That was it. He left, and I've never seen him since. Immediately the devil started working on my mind saying that it was just a coincidence. *Are you kidding me?!* No one will ever be able to explain that one away. That is no coincidence! He just appeared like Melchizedek did to Abraham in Genesis 14 only to encourage him and never be heard from again. What an amazing God we serve that He can use any random person with impeccable timing so precisely to speak to me and my particular situation. If that man had not been mindful of what God wanted to do through him, that night would have just been an ordinary night out shopping for him. It would have been an average night at work for me. I might have continued to be frustrated and doubtful when I went home that night. But it was not ordinary for me, and I pray he went home encouraged that God was using him. I would have never had the conversation the next morning with my wife that encouraged me to go downstairs and write this chapter if that man had not kept his mind open to hear God and been obedient to what God was saying.

To make it even better, I had been reading the book of Esther and came to the realization that, once the timing was right, God moved very swiftly. Mordecai went from being a marked man with a death sentence to leaving the king's presence wearing royal garments in one day (Esther chapters 5-8). If you read the whole book a couple of times, you'll see that Esther was put into a place to be an advocate for the Jews not because of her beauty, but because of God's favor and timing. She knew what she was supposed to do and recognized the opportunity but chapter 4:12-14 records a moment where she needed to be encouraged. Had Mordecai not been mindful of God's ability to control a situation and encouraged Esther, she might have lost hope and given up. The two work together so beautifully that God's ultimate plan of freedom for the suppressed Jews was a success through Haman's death (the last of the Amalekites, which fulfilled Exodus 17:15).

God put that person in my life at that time for a reason! That's the kind of God I serve!

God is omniscient (Isaiah 46:9-10). That means He knows, comprehends, and understands all things with divine wisdom that reaches much deeper than our own. *Any problem you have, He knows a plan that will fix it!*

God is omnipotent (Daniel 4:35). That means He can do things and undo things that we cannot even imagine. *If there is an obstacle holding you back, He can move it!*

God is omnipresent (Jeremiah 23:24). That means His spirit is with us anywhere we go. *Wherever you go, He goes!*

Something even more pleasant than those things is that who God goes so much further than being all-powerful, all-knowing, and everywhere at all times. He loves you with a love you can never fully comprehend, and He wants the best for you even more than you want it for yourself. He can move mountains and calm the wind and waves but only when you learn to give Him full control. You owe it to yourself to become mindful of His presence in your life. When you don't trust Him, you are preventing His unobstructed work in your life. I was going to finish this chapter with a paragraph about what God can do and how He can do it, but the bottom line is that it does not matter *how* He works. All that matters is that He does work and wants to work and will work. I don't understand how a microwave works, but I'm glad it does (or I would not have eaten much as a child)! The words of the old hymn Trust and Obey by John H. Sammis say it best: "Trust and obey, for there's no other way to be happy in Jesus but to trust and obey."

Practice Point: Stop reading this book for a few seconds and look beside you. Imagine that the God whom you serve is sitting with you. What would you say to Him? How would you act? What would you offer Him as a gracious host? Read Ephesians 3:14-21 and fully embrace that God is able.

CHAPTER 5

SATAN CAN'T!

WHEN YOU WRAP YOUR head around everything that God is and what His Word teaches, you begin to realize that Satan's power is insignificant when compared to God's provision. *Satan has no power except what we give him.* However, he does have a plan, and we must know our enemy's plan and understand how he works. We will get into that soon, but the first step in realizing that Satan cannot stop you is in grasping a righteous and Biblical understanding of who he is and what his motive is. I don't like to think of him as "the devil" as it seems to minimize an accurate view of him. That term is thrown around so much that it no longer represents his true character. Some sports teams proudly call themselves devils. They must think that word means something that is robust and powerful, fast and furious, even tenacious. Movies and music make the devil seem almost fun and childish, almost cartoon-like.

That is not at all who "the devil" is.

The reason he roams like a lion seeking to devour (1 Peter 5:8) is that we have something he wants, and he can never have. He is jealous, and jealous people want to hurt the ones who are not suffering. He is a perverter of the truth, a thief of dreams, a murderer of hopes, a destroyer of love. He wants to wreck your life. He wants nothing less than to tear you away from the One who loves you most. He is the king of hate and that's all he does. He hates everything and everyone (most likely even himself). Satan despises you and wants you to fail. He knows the only way for you to fail is when he can distract you so that you lose faith in what God can do.

Like a child that is jealous when another kid has something he wants, so Satan is jealous of what you have in Christ.

Satan knows that his rebellion separated him from God permanently. That is his judgment. He messed up and cannot be redeemed, so his only motive is to take you down with him. Second Corinthians 11:14 tells us that "Satan masquerades as an angel of light." *His only weapon is deception.* If he can deceive you into thinking you've messed up too much or that God doesn't love you or that you will never be used by God, then he wins. He wins if and when he distracts you from God's plan for your life. He likes to use fear, but fear is simply deception that something you don't fully understand will harm you. If the lights are turned off and you're home alone, and you hear a strange loud bang, it may frighten you because you don't know what it is. Somewhere along the way, we have learned to think the worst first. However, if you know someone else is home or you have heard your furnace make weird noises like that previously, or you are aware that someone is working on the roof, the sound likely won't garner your attention as you are more likely to attribute the noise to one of those sources. If the lights were on and you saw the cat jump off the table and knock a book onto the floor, you would know that you had no reason to be afraid at all. It may still startle you, but you would be silly actually to succumb to fear for your life over that sound.

I don't mean to sound corny or cliché here but Jesus is your light, many scriptures say so. When you train yourself to be mindful that He is there with you, you will have nothing to fear. In Joshua 1:9 we are reminded not to be terrified or discouraged because the Lord our God is with us wherever we go. Satan wants you to turn off Jesus Christ's light in your life. He wants you to feel like you're all alone so that when he brings something into your life that shakes things up a bit, you feel like there is no one to turn to, and you become afraid. When Jesus was tempted in the desert (recorded in Matthew chapter 4), He responded with scripture. Satan had no choice but to leave.

Satan could not distract Jesus because Jesus knew that God is the only one with any real authority.

Don't' fall for the fake! Satan knows your weak points. I do not believe that he can control your mind unless you give him authority to do so. I do think that he can put the proverbial carrot in front of the horse and hope that you follow it. In my opinion, he is like a fisher using attractive baits. The outcome is masterfully hidden. The unsuspecting fish that sees the yummy treat does not know it will soon be filleted and eaten. All it wants is that shiny chartreuse spinner bait! *In the same way, when a good enough imitation of God's best is offered, we often fall for it.* At work, I often have to remind my clients (we call them guests) that; getting drunk or high to relieve stress or pain just comes down to giving into an imitation of what God has outlined in His Word. They say themselves that the pain is still there when they wake up.

My God will take that stress away completely. Having a

sexually active relationship outside of the boundaries of marriage is, again, an imitation of God's best for your life. That action becomes more about indulging into selfish, lustful desires than experiencing love by fulfilling another person's needs. Imitation foods and fragrances are never quite the same as the real thing because they are not made of the real ingredients. Those imitations will never fulfill you the way the authentic product does because it's just tricking of your senses. Jesus offers the real plan of love and salvation. His plan is the only one that will work, and He will bear the burden with you and make your troubles lighter! Do not fall for the imitations and lies. Second Corinthians 10:4-5 says, "The weapons we fight with are not the weapons of the world. On the contrary, they have divine power to demolish strongholds. We demolish arguments and every pretension that sets itself up against the knowledge of God, and we take captive every thought to make it obedient to Christ."

As I stated earlier, the devil has no power unless we give it to him. There is no reason to fear him. He is a small, measly, powerless creature that is casting an enormous shadow against the wall. He does not rule hell. Hell is a judgment place set aside for him and those he deceives. He doesn't rule anything. When we learn to see him for who he is and see ourselves for who God empowered us to be, we win. I often read back through the stories of Peter and Judas Iscariot. They were both strong men of God (at least at some points in their lives) who walked with Jesus, but their closely paralleled stories have dramatically different endings.

I'm sure most of you know the story of how Judas sold the secret of where Jesus was for a little bit of money and then hanged himself afterward. The truth is Jesus was not hiding and would have made his location known all by Himself if need be. Unfortunately, Judas forgot that no sin is too big for God to forgive and remove. He went back to the chief priests and gave the money back and confessed to them. "What is that to us?" the Bible records them asking in Matthew 27:4. They did not care. He should have run to Jesus. Yes, Judas betrayed Him, but I bet our Savior would have embraced Judas with a big hug and only told him to go and sin no more (as He had said in the story we already discussed in John 8). How sad it is that Judas, who spent so much time physically next to our Christ, so quickly forgot all the teachings of forgiveness. He did what we often do: he pronounced his own judgment upon himself. Judas was probably sitting in the crowd when Jesus said: "Do not judge, or you too will be judged" (Matthew 7:1), yet he made the decision to be his final judge.

I believe that Peter's story could have ended the same way as Judas.' However, after he denied Christ and heard the rooster, he did not carry out a sentence upon himself. Peter "wept bitterly" (Matthew 26:74) in repentance. He must have decided that, as hard as it may be, he was going to come clean and repent because he was with the other disciples when Jesus returned. He went on to write books that encouraged believers in a dark time of persecution. *Listen friends: your greatest failure does not have to define the rest of your life!* You have to make the decision to get up off the ground, dust yourself off, and go back in the fight. The only determining difference in these two stories is that one held it all in and the let it all out.

We cannot condemn ourselves! That's how Satan wins!

Satan wants you to think that it's too late, but you have to learn to cut his hook from your mouth. In Ephesians 4:27 Paul said: "and do not give the devil a foothold." I like the word "give" there. Satan cannot *take* it. Those lures really distract us. That is why we should warn teenagers to avoid the Ouija board and be careful of what movies or music that they hear and see. Proverbs 5:22 says "The evil deeds of the wicked ensnare them; the cords of their sins hold them fast." Matthew 12:35 says "A good man brings good things out of the good stored up in him, and an evil man brings evil things out of the evil stored up in him."

Your eyes and ears are windows to your spirit, and you must be ever mindful of those open windows. I picture our spirit like a little child living inside of us. Whenever you are divulging in sinful acts, I see that spirit covering its ears and closing its eyes. I imagine it saying, "please stop, please stop" and hovering in the corner like a child hiding in her room when her parents are arguing. Eventually, the Holy Spirit's convicting nudge has to leave. God cannot be around anything impure! David understood that God had to hide from our transgressions, or he would not have stated that, "If I had cherished sin in my heart, the Lord would not have listened." (Psalm 66:18). Other versions state it differently; "If I had not confessed the sin in my heart, the Lord would not have listened." (NLT) "If I regard iniquity in my heart, the Lord will not hear me." (KJV) I believe these simple variations still relay the same message. We cannot allow sin to own a place in our hearts that is higher than God's. I believe these verses remind us that God cannot come near sin and thus sin breaks that intimate relationship which God wants to have with each of us!

Convincing us to replace God's best with our selfish acts is Satan's greatest weapon.

Get the sin out of your life so you can be connected to what God is trying to tell you. Satan understands this better than any of us and will attack our mind but that's the extent of his limits. *Our prayers and our faith in God will keep Satan's authority at bay*. God will not allow him to mess with us beyond what we can bear.

Traditionally, I've heard Christians say God controls everything and when anything goes wrong it's either due to a lack of faith or God permitting the devil to "test us." I have to say that I don't believe that as a general rule. I understand there are generational curses and problems we bring upon ourselves, but those things can change when we call on the name of Jesus. That's the whole purpose of the crucifixion, not just to make a way for us to be in heaven, but to break all of Satan's power and free us even while we're alive here on the earth.

Does God allow the earthquake that kills thousands? Was it God's will for the tragedy of September 11th? I don't believe so. Jesus warned us that the earth would wear out like a garment. His Word tells us of wars and rumors of wars and people turning against each other. That is the unfortunate nature of an imperfect world and impure society. That's why there will be a new heaven and earth when sin is judged and cast away. As was stated in the previous chapter, God has the power to protect us, and I believe He is constantly trying to warn us of the things surrounding us *if we become ever mindful.* I know some of you may be thinking, "well, what about Job?" God was in control the whole time, and He must have known Job could bear the trials. I don't believe God brings all trials upon us for a particular purpose, but I do think he provides the strength and resources for us to learn something valuable in those times.

As Kirk Franklin says, God turns our test into our testimony!

God is right there watching over you the whole time, and He loves you. He does not want any harm to come to you. Satan may seem intimidating but just run to God, and you'll have the strength you need to get through anything. Proverbs 18:10 tells us that "The name of the Lord is a strong tower; the righteous man runs into it and is safe." (ESV) Friends, run to the safety and protection of God's tower. When you are afraid, when you're in doubt, when you're worried, remember that God can and Satan can't! Give yourself a break and rest in God until you have the answer you need.

Practice Point: Stop for a few moments and simply rest in God. Let go of your fears. Let go of those imitations to which you have succumbed. Tell that rascally Satan that he has no place in your life and you will not fall for his tricks! Read James 4:7 out loud!! (We will take this further in the next chapter.)

CHAPTER 6

TRUE REPENTANCE

IF WE EVER WANT to see God move in our lives, we cannot go on pretending that sinful behavior can just be overlooked. One of the biggest keys to living a life that is "ever mindful" is to understand regular self-evaluation and turning away from those behaviors which inhibit forward spiritual progress. How is it that we have come so far that many of us just accept sin? Sin is the only thing that separates us from the One who loves us most? It is a wall that blocks us from being in His presence yet we go on as if it does not exist. We laugh at lewd jokes; we watch movies that blaspheme our God; we allow things to be a part of our lives that should not be there. Why? We must learn to hate sin and stand against it! It is disgusting, sickening, degrading, annoying, disturbing, vile, tormenting, limiting. We must pray that God helps us to get passionate about this.

No one likes to talk about sin. The word itself is cringe-worthy. However, sins of the heart (such as a bad attitude, ungratefulness, unforgiveness, and being spiteful, etc.) are just as spiritually debilitating as any other sins which are more outwardly noticeable. I believe that, in everyone's life, there is a time to fully confront the things in our past and present that are not ok with God. It is not my place to tell you everything that is or is not sin, but you must get in your quiet place with God and ask Him to reveal these things. It is important that we are often re-examining ourselves and turning to God for help with the things we have said or done that have hurt others or hurt God. When we hold on to this stuff, we can push God away. To truly repent means three basic things: You must recognize Jesus Christ had to pay the price for you (Romans 5:8). Confess your sins to Him. Finally, ask for forgiveness by welcoming Christ's blood to wash away your grievances. First John 1:9 says "If we confess our sins, he is faithful and just and will forgive us our sins and purify us from all unrighteousness." That word, "confess," in the original Hebrew is "homologeo." It can also be translated as "acknowledge." I believe this means that we do not have to go around telling everyone all the wrong things we have done. I believe it means we simply come to terms with our wrongdoing. Admitting any wrong is the first step, and everything after that is a lot easier as you will have already started forward progress.

It never hurts to make it right with someone that you may have offended either. Intentionally turn away from those unhealthy things and believe that you are forgiven (Romans 10:8-10) A farmer who has found thistles in his land must dig them out and allow that ground to dry out before it can be used again. Is your heart a pure ground? There is a sickness of the blood called Sepsis. It is a serious, life threatening infection that starts small and gets worse very quickly. Because it affects your blood, it infects your entire body very quickly and 28 to 50% of those infected die (according to the National Institute of General Medical Sciences). It can be detected early and treated and the patient will go on to a normal, healthy life, but only if it's treated quickly. Sin is the sepsis of spiritual growth.

Sin has to be dealt with before it spreads and causes you to hurt the ones you love most.

True repentance is a process. As you read stories of repentance in the Bible, you'll see the process was always very personal, and there was often a sacrifice given. I believe that the reason the Israelites had to bring an animal to be sacrificed for their sin is that God wanted it to be personal. The Old Testament Day of Atonement was not a fun time. I am sure the early Israelites remembered this day when they were tempted to go against God's Word. During a time of repentance, the people would even dress in sackcloth and put ashes on their skin to show the outward sign of the death and mourning that was going on inside. I am thankful that Jesus Christ paid that sacrifice for us once and for all so we don't have to do that now, but I'm afraid it's just too easy to apologize and move on when we've missed the mark. *We must understand that our sin creates tension between our spirit and God's and it cannot live within us any longer.*

I'm sure you know by now that temptation does not disappear just because you repent. God knew the power of allowing the pagan lifestyle to remain in the camp when He commanded the Israelites in Deuteronomy 7:2 "and when the Lord your God has delivered them over to you, and you have defeated them, then you must destroy them totally. Make no treaty with them, and show them no mercy." There are countless warnings in the Bible in almost every book against allowing the remnants of sin to hang around. We are, unfortunately, amenable people, and we get off track very easily. When you are finally ready to change a bad habit in your life, it is not enough to repent. You need to know why it's wrong, maybe even write it down in a private journal so that you can reference it when you feel like throwing in the towel. We make excuses such as: "it's fun, I like it, it's exciting, it makes me feel good, I don't have anything to look forward to," but in doing this, we are only lying to ourselves.

The bottom line is that God commanded us to purge sin from our lives for a reason, and we better listen!

Sin destroys everything in its path. It takes and never gives back. You may not be able to see the ill-effects immediately, but that is only because you are blinded by the temporary gratitude (going back to the previous chapter and the discussion about imitations). *God knows where He's leading you, and your sin is your only obstacle.* Get those roadblocks out of the way so you can remain on His path and see the permanent blessings. When we give in to unforgiveness or start creating tension, when we act arrogantly or respond to people harshly, we are allowing our flesh to win the battle over the spirit. Our sinful nature is rooted in darkness and is void of God's love. (Psalm 51:5, "Surely I was sinful at birth, sinful from the time my mother conceived me.") If you permit me to use anthropomorphic terms for the flesh, I will say the following: Your flesh wants you to cower away from what is right because it fears being exposed. Your flesh is constantly at war with what is righteous and holy.

Your flesh is a part of you that must be addressed regularly.

When you start consciously working on the faults in your life, it will bring you closer to the One who can reveal more to you. Then you work on more things, and that brings you closer to God. Satan's lies will not easily fool you when you remain close to God. That doesn't mean you have to be perfect right now, but make a conscious effort to begin to change. One of my favorite scriptures is Matthew 4:20 "At once they left their nets and followed him." I like it because it represents the idea of leaving everything behind and following Jesus only because He said so. Those disciples knew they would have nothing to return to if they left their nets. They knew they were stepping into the unknown. Their lives were changed because of it. When we become ever mindful of what God is trying to do and why He's doing it, a habit of immediately acting on what He's telling us to do will form.

True repentance only works when it is coupled with discipline.

Before we go any further, I think it's important that you really take a moment to recognize the price that was paid for your sin and thank Jesus for it. Ask God to forgive you and help you be better. If you've never officially asked Jesus to be in your heart, please take a moment and do it now. It doesn't have to be a fancy prayer, just say something like this: "Jesus, I'm sorry, forgive me, help me, I invite you in my heart." Start looking for a Bible-based church that helps you walk in His ways and you'll be well on your way to becoming ever mindful!

Now is a good time to pause take a good look at your purity scale. What is standing in your way that you can control? Pretend there is a string with a weight on either end hanging evenly off your index finger. The string represents your mind. One side represents the sinful mindset and the other represents closeness to God's perfect will. You can pull it all the way down on either side, but that means it is shorter on the other. On which side would your string be the longest?

Ask God, what He is trying to tell you that you may not be hearing and doing? In what areas of your life have you shut God out? I keep thinking of my daughter trying to tell me something or get my attention to play a game with her while I'm too busy watching a football game or engaged in another conversation. She will eventually give up and play by herself. But what's great about her is what's great about God, when I come to my senses and decide to turn my attention to her, she's excited again and ready to go. I think that's how the Holy Spirit is in our lives. Ask God to help you. *Let your selfish ambitions and your motives die.* Let your agenda fade. That's when God can go to work.

Once you begin to recognize your shortcomings and learn how to fix some of them, you'll notice some things that you just can't fight on your own. When you are face to face with a behavior in your life that you do not like, but cannot outrun, you must call for backup. I saw a movie once where a group of soldiers was cut off and saw no way out. They called on the radio a code word and immediately there were jet planes all around them giving support. You must find someone that you can call in these times of weakness. Find a trusted friend or person of God that will be honest with you. You must be able to speak openly and describe what sets you off and exactly what your reaction is. Discuss ways of beating this behavior. Ask them to be your backup.

I've found that if there is no consequence for my actions, I don't change anything.

I customize a plan that hits home for me. You will have to discover a routine that will work for you. It can be something as simple as not allowing yourself to watch your favorite TV show if you fail again, or maybe you have to spend an extra 30 minutes reading your Bible or fast a meal the next time you slip up (don't look at it as punishment though). Your plan must be straightforward and documented with your accountability partner so they can follow up with you. A buddy and I used to have an agreement where we called each other every Tuesday morning and asked very direct questions that left no room for ambiguity. If I slipped up, I had to tell him, and he would remind me of my consequence. Our penalty was that we had to turn off the video games for a week. I know it seems juvenile, but when something you enjoy is on the line, it provides some motivation.

Now, you could argue that you're only staying disciplined because of the punishment but my response is that you should do whatever it takes. No matter how simple or futile your motivation for remaining ever mindful is, it will build healthy habits. Many times you just need to change the behavior for a little while. Then you come to the realization that God's way is better, and you don't want the old ways anymore. It's kind of like starting a diet. I used to eat white bread and drink cola and eat cheeseburgers way too often, but the more I replaced that stuff with healthy foods, it's funny how I didn't want to eat that junk so much anymore.

Practice Point: Say this statement out loud, *"I am walking in purity. I am a spotless bride before Christ! Nothing is holding me back from being who God wants me to be."* If you take this seriously, you are not only claiming this over your life (see Proverbs 18:21), but you are also inviting the Holy Spirit to speak to you regarding whatever is holding you back. If you are like I was at the time I originally wrote this, get a pen and a lot of paper so that you can write down what the Holy Spirit is telling you. Look at your list, mark the date, and take this seriously. (This way, you won't move on too quickly and forget it.) Today begins a new you; a birthday of sorts!

CHAPTER 7

DISCIPLINE LEADS TO DISCIPLINE

IF YOU JUST SAID the prayer of repentance or took some time to write out things you want to change about yourself (from the end of the previous chapter), please know that this decision should be paired with voluntary commitment. You do not have to be perfect in this, but it should be your highest priority to make some effort. It's not always easy to pray and read your Bible or go to church regularly, but those things should become a vital part of your life. Again, becoming ever mindful is about keeping a Christ-focused lifestyle as your number one priority at all times. As a Christian, God's Word should be front and foremost. I often think of people I admire in my life and wonder how they can love so selflessly or give so cheerfully, or even just remain dedicated to their dream steadfastly. I've had the pleasure of asking some of them how they do it. The common response is surprising. I have heard from more than one person who say that, even after years of living that way, those traits still do not come naturally. I even heard one say that it is still difficult for him to be that way but he knows it is important. Friends, how do we become the people we want to be? How do we get to a place where we can sense God's gentle nudge in the busiest and craziest of times?

From personal experience, the only thing I know is that this lifestyle takes discipline.

Discipline is a homonym (two or more words which are spelled the same and sound the same but have different meanings). It can mean working hard and being dedicated and it can also mean the act of teaching or enforcing acceptable behaviors. For the first half of this chapter, I want to discuss the word discipline based upon the definition by Dictionary.com which states that it is "a regimen that develops or improves a skill." Through many years of praying to be more disciplined, I've come to realize that it's not something you *get* but more something you choose to *do*. It does not usually come naturally. Simply put, it is a choice to be disciplined in your thoughts and actions.

When you want something enough, the prospect of having it should outweigh any disgruntlement you may feel during the times of sacrifice that are required for you to achieve it. Regarding becoming ever mindful of God's guidance, following His plan over your desires will lead to the fruit of the spirit coming out of you more naturally (see Galatians 5:22-23). Now is a good time to concentrate on the difference between verbs and nouns. I'm sure you know that a verb is an action word, and a noun is a person, place, or thing. Obviously, some words can be used either way. Discipline is certainly one of those words. Discipline is certainly a noun, in terms of something you can possess. For now, I want you to think of discipline in the context of a verb, something you intentionally do…A CHOICE.

Have you ever been promoted at work, or had some other good fortune, only to find that the ones who should be most excited for you are jealous? If you have ever had this happen in your life, you likely saw certain people begin to despise you and even become bitter towards you. In my experience, many times these people neglect to look inward and ask themselves if they should work harder or follow instructions better. They would rather spend their efforts playing the blame game or discussing how lucky you are. I always find it strange when people are so quick to blame their upbringing or their family life or bad luck when the real problem is their lack of discipline. In my life, I know it is easy to make an excuse which places the blame on a lack of money, talent, or even my family while never doing any sort of self-evaluation.

Making excuses will only cause us to focus on the negative instead of asking God how to help the situation.

Often, a simple tweak in one or two areas would make a dramatic impact, but we never see how simple it is because the sour attitude blinds us. Sometimes it takes more patience than I'm willing to give. Philippians 2:14 "Do everything without complaining or arguing." Matthew 12:36 +37 "But I tell you that everyone will have to give account on the day of judgment for every empty word they have spoken. For by your words you will be acquitted, and by your words you will be condemned." Now don't fear that God won't allow you to talk about your feelings, but we must be careful as those feelings can quickly shape our attitude. I believe that it is ok to vent to God a little now and then; but we must do it respectfully. I love it when my daughter lets me know what's bothering her because that is the only way I can help her. God does care about your worries; that trait is what is so beautiful about Him. It's pointless to whine and grumble for too long because it gets your mind off track. To combat this, discipline in your thought life is paramount.

We must understand that the devil knows this as well, and our carnal flesh would rather complain than make adjustments.

I guess that, by now, you have begun to realize that the process of becoming ever mindful does not stop at just being self-aware. I can be coherent enough to see a stop light ahead of me but, if I'm not obedient to the laws of the land, it doesn't matter, right? When I see the light turn red and know that means I should take my foot off the gas pedal, it's still a conscious effort on my part actually to stop the car. In the same way, we can get to the place where we recognize God's voice and even get good at stopping and listening to it, but we must also make the right choice. If God is telling you to do something and you hear Him and understand Him but are not doing it, you are not obedient, and you are not ever mindful. James 4:17 (which you should have read as a practice point at the end of chapter 5) reminds us to "Submit yourselves, then, to God. Resist the devil, and he will flee from you.." Keep in mind the obvious implication that obedience is also a choice.

As you make the choice to become more disciplined, obedience should follow in kind.

Now, I want to discuss the word discipline based upon its use which implies correction. I know that many of my best character traits were brought upon through being disciplined as a child. At the time of being disciplined, I looked at it as a negative thing as I was being deprived of something I wanted as a response to something I was not supposed to be doing. I do believe God disciplines His people in some ways; although it is not always easy to identify. I notice God's discipline in my life through the form of conviction. The feeling that something is just not right is often my first comprehension of the Holy Spirit nudging me towards or away from a decision. God sets parameters of how we should behave which is why He disciplines us. It is silly to presume that God disciplines us for any reason other than that which is for our good. *Throughout the scriptures, it is apparent that God loves His people enough to correct them when they are going off-course.* We cannot fully understand His way of discipline because it comes from true love. The boundaries that He has set are not because He wants to keep us in a box. He knows the difference between freedom and slavery on a whole different level.

When I discipline my daughter, I have to recognize that my reasoning is imperfect. I punish my daughter because she does not see how one wrong act can lead to a habit. She doesn't realize that the reason I make her hold my hand when crossing the street is to avoid the dangers inherent (she has never had to face the reality of that hazard). All her mind tells her is that I'm trying to restrain her free spirit. I can explain that she has to wear her hat and gloves when going out in the snow, but she doesn't get it until her fingers and ears are freezing from being exposed to the cold. Although I hope to discipline based upon what is best for her, my thoughts are tarnished by imperfection. Comparatively, God is perfect in His very nature and does not have this obstacle in His path. My response to a situation can only be based on my experiences, but God's rests on perfect love.

God does not discipline His people for any reason other than to draw them closer to Himself.

It's great to have a solid understanding of those two explanations of discipline, but what's next? I believe it is crucial that we respond to God's discipline (the second meaning) with discipline (the first meaning). God has rules because He knows what the other side holds. He knows how one wrong decision can dramatically affect the rest of your life, and He sets the rules on what is sin in your life and disciplines accordingly because He wants you to make better decisions before you find out the hard way. Our Lord knows your individual strengths and weaknesses. So, if you're dealing with a "gray area" in your life (something the Scriptures tell you is wrong, and you're not sure why) just remind yourself what God says and that He knows best. His ways ARE higher than ours. He DOES know more than we. He ALWAYS has your best interest in mind. Why is this so difficult to grasp? Why do we still follow our selfish ambitions even when we know they take us down the path we do not want to follow? I can only speak for myself here, but I believe the key is humility. I will elaborate on this over the remainder of this chapter.

The only reason I can think of for which I would take my path over God's "good, pleasing and perfect will" (according to Romans 12:2), is because of my arrogance. I'm not sure about anyone else, but my perception of a situation is rarely the best outlook. Let's think about our perceptions for a moment. I do admit that it's almost impossible to look at a situation and not judge it based on the first appearance. I certainly notice this when meeting someone new. In those first few seconds, my mind is often racing with opinions. Unfortunately, the first couple of thoughts that run through my mind are motivated by my history. It 's hard to see through the eyes of the Creator. Have you ever noticed someone change their tone when speaking to an attractive person, or to their boss, or someone else that they respect? *It's interesting how we often create different personas based on our prejudices or biases.* I often remember a time when I was selling life insurance and making cold calls from home. My wife overheard me talking to a prospective client in a much kinder voice than she was used to hearing from me. When I hung up the phone, she asked me why I didn't talk to her like that. Good question. Whatever the answer, it's not sufficient. Fortunately,

God is not like that; He does not change for anyone.

He does not choose favorites and decide if He wants to be kind or harsh today. He does not discipline you according to a perception. *His discipline is for one reason and one reason only: love.* The Bible even warns us that we cannot grasp this love. His only intent is to equip us to get back to Him and bring others with us. It was upon this realization that I came to this conclusion: if God loves me and only sets rules because of His love for me then I have no reason to follow a contradictory path. Romans chapter 6 records how we've been set free from the slavery of sin. You must be mindful that even when you have repented of the old lifestyle, God will have to discipline the continuation of sin. He can only do this if we learn to live a life of humility. He does not send people to hell because He wants to. *God's discipline is because He loves you and wants to be reunited with you in Heaven after this life is over.*

Practice Point: Think of a few areas in your life where you can be much more disciplined. Write out a plan and talk to a trusted friend so that you remain dedicated to changing this behavior. Look at it again in a month and evaluate your progress. Repeat as necessary!

CHAPTER 8

DISCIPLINE LEADS TO HUMILITY

WITH DISCIPLINE FRESH ON your mind, let us now focus on humility. I believe that we can never discover God's best for our lives until we humble ourselves and line up with His plan. When we make decisions outside of the restraints of humility, they can change the whole course of our lives! Often, we would rather take matters into our hands instead of asking God and waiting for His timing. This impatience can be a sign of arrogance. We must get back to the humility Jesus represented. He had no earthly reason to put any person's wants, needs, or requests above His own; but He continually did that (when they lined up with God's will for their life, of course). He was always found hanging out with the unwanted or allowing Himself to be interrupted or using everyday situations to teach valuable lessons.

Jesus purposely entered into conversations where the receiver's life could be better.

I can only speak for myself in regards to humility. On my journey of becoming ever mindful of what God has in store for me, I have had to re-examine my motives. In my life, I can be very arrogant and extremely impatient (just ask my wife). If I have an idea, and someone else offers a different opinion, I often run right through whatever advice they are giving because I like my way better. Often, when my wife calls for me to help her with something I holler back "just a minute" because I want to be in control of when and what I do. (I now notice my daughter responding this way…yikes!) Sometimes, when I'm having a conversation that's not centered on what I want, I check out and look for a way to end the conversation. If I care about the other person's idea more than my own, I will listen more. I understand that this behavior tells the other person that their time or ideas are not important to me. When someone asks me to do something, and I don't agree with their reason, I grumble and complain. That is a distinct lack of humility (a lack of discipline), and I have to admit it, repent of it, and make it right.

As I read how Jesus invited interruptions in the New Testament, it makes me think of how I would have reacted in those situations.

Would I have sat down by the woman at the well? Would I have stopped in a large crowd and turned to the one woman with an issue of blood that grabbed for me? Jesus was clearly not annoyed by those interruptions. He was humble enough to recognize other people even when He had a busy schedule. I sure wish I was as comfortable with interruptions as He was. More humility would certainly help. I am excellent at being kind and thoughtful when I'm in a group setting or at church or when I'm with a client at work. I will even put others ahead of myself in those situations. What I really don't like about myself is that, when it does not benefit me in some way, rarely am I as loving and giving. I hate that. I can play with the kids at a family gathering for a while, but, when I'm getting bored with it, I start to complain. Then I whine to my wife about why nobody else plays with the kids to give me a break. In these times, I am learning that I need to stop and evaluate my motivation.

True humility will naturally be paired with sacrifice (which means it is not always easy).

It's not a sacrifice until you give something of importance. I am magnificent at having my devotion time with God when I have about twenty minutes before I have to leave for work. However, I'm atrocious at it when I have the whole day off to do whatever I want. I know that it's because there is not much I can do with a smaller amount of time so I don't mind *sacrificing* it. When I have the whole day ahead of me, there are so many other things that I can do…like watch a movie or play a video game or play my drums (you know, critical things). Another big thing I have noticed in my life is that I am great at asking God to help me, but not so great at accepting His help.

When I first started writing this book, I was living with my in-laws (as I spoke of in my introduction) and often got upset with God because I didn't have my place yet. I would say things like, "I have always done things the right way, and put church first and worked hard, why can't you help me out" as if my acts should have earned a special blessing. A humble spirit would instead thank Him for the people that would take my family in on short notice and put up with having a dog in their house. I felt entitlement because I had lived the "Christian" life. I had to suck up my pride and learn to be humble. I know I would not have learned these things if this situation did not happen in my life. *There is always a conflict when we feel entitlement in any situation with God.* This prideful attitude means that I feel I have done something to earn what I have or be where I am, but God "shows favor to the humble…" (Proverbs 3:34) I often hear pastors say that Christ's death on the cross provided unmerited favor. I like it stated in that way. If that's correct, He did it regardless of my actions. I did not have to ask him. God even went as far as granting me the faith to recognize and receive it. I did not deserve it. I did not have to do anything. In this way, Jesus modeled true humility. He did something purely for the good of someone else. He did not do this so that He could brag about it.

Unless we are truly and utterly humble, and in a place where we are responding to God's discipline regularly, I would suggest that God will rarely use us. It's one thing to say you're humble or try to be a servant, but we must wholly adopt the attitude. So how can we fix this? How do we begin the path of recognition? I think it is very simple. We must get to a place where we habitually ask God to help us recognize pride in our lives. We must get to the place where we take upon ourselves the necessary discipline to humbly submit to God's Word. Trust me; He will honor that submission. When we admit our wrong, we are already learning humility.

I believe that being honest and not making excuses is the hardest part.

Understanding that you are in control of your choices should actually give you freedom. You can choose to be humble in most situations. A choice to DO something also means NOT doing another thing. Being ever mindful is a choice. It is something that you "willfully" do (or do not do). A choice to get up and go to church on a Sunday morning is also a choice to not sleep in or get caught up on house cleaning. *God honors Christlike choices.* He will bless the person who is honoring Him with their choices. Think of the choice you made when you decided what career to begin. That decision made other choices possible or not possible. You may wish now that you would have made other choices. I am finding that I'm getting pretty good at being ever mindful, but that's probably only because I look at this almost daily. Unfortunately, that does not always equal being obedient (as we viewed earlier). Many times I know I should not be acting the way I am in a given situation, but I don't actually change anything. What is the point of being mindful if I am not also continually pushing myself towards the goal through discipline and humility? I have touched on this a little already, but it is worth saying again. The only answer to this dilemma is humility. Discipline leads to humility which is not something we naturally *have*. It is something we *DO*.

Being humble means making a sacrifice for one thing because you believe more in another thing.

Often, until we face something terrible as a result of our neglect, we don't usually care. Humility will change that. I often have conversations with our guests at work that have decided to change their behavior only because their life cannot get much worse. An outside source has humbled them. If they had only humbled themselves at an earlier stage in their lives and asked for help, their situation might not have turned out so grim. I don't have to see my daughter fall out of a tree to know that climbing it isn't safe, but when it comes to matters of the mind and heart, the cause and effect isn't always so apparent. *It all comes down to one question: what are you willing to sacrifice?* There will be things that are in the gray area, but you know what God asks of you. In regards to a sinful or otherwise corrupt attitude sometimes it just comes down to not doing something because it is getting in the way. We cannot respond with, "that's just the way I am." That is thinking with an unpurified, undisciplined, arrogant mind. We are not allowed to use that as an excuse if we claim to be Christians. Since being a Christian means we are "of or like Christ," we should say, "that's the way I used to be, I may struggle with that, but God is working on me."

Practice Point: Examine some areas in your life where you could start responding with more humility. I suggest that you do something nice for someone for no particular reason. Buy a coffee or candy bar for someone. Give someone a big hug. Make a phone call just to say hi. These baby steps can lead to a lifestyle of humility!

CHAPTER 9

FORM YOUR VISION

ONCE YOU WRAP YOUR head around being disciplined and humble, you can start forming your vision. Most importantly, you can line up your vision with what God's Word is revealing to you regarding His plan for you. Becoming ever mindful just comes down to finding your motivation and having the self-discipline and determination to follow your dreams and goals without allowing distractions to pull you away. Having a vision gives you a true north to keep yourself focused. Of course, I don't mean a vision of some apparition in the sky or a theophany of Jesus Christ. I'm talking about a mental picture of where you want to be and what you want to be doing. In chapter 3 "How God Sees You," we explored changing our mindset and seeing ourselves through God's eyes. When you grasp an understanding of that, you will start making decisions differently.

Your personal vision of what God can do through your talents, gifts, and opportunities should be clearly stated.

If you have been working on the practice points, hopefully, you have established some basics of what you believe. Maybe you have even begun to turn away from some of the junk that's holding you back in life. If you take this a step further and begin to examine ways God can use you, you are on an amazing track! It is necessary that you have something to hope in before you can envision it coming true. I'm sure you've heard the term, "Don't get your hopes up, or you'll be disappointed." That is extremely contrary to God's word. Once again Satan uses broad society to convince us that it's normal to be drab, boring, and doubtful. God says that it is okay to get your hopes up. He encourages us many times to activate our faith and believe in the improbable. Paul attributes God as someone who "is able to do immeasurably more than all we ask or imagine, according to his power that is at work within us," in Ephesians 3:20. I don't know about you, but I can imagine a lot of things. God can do more than that! This was Paul's prayer for the people of the church of Ephesus, and he was speaking of God's immense love for His people. *Someone who loves you that much would probably want you to get your hopes WAY UP!!*

The Bible includes many scriptures that deal directly with having hope. One of my favorites is Hebrews 6:19a "We have this hope as an anchor for the soul, firm and secure." In the same way that an anchor holds a ship in place during the worst of storms, so our hope keeps us in place when the going gets tough. When the storms of life come crashing in, our anchor (the hope in our God's guidance) can keep our mind focused. The next part is the disappointment. I believe you are only disappointed when things don't go the way *you* think they should go. If you learn to place your hope in *the Provider* instead of *the provision*, then you will know that if God doesn't work things out the way you wanted, then He must have a better plan.

Don't worry about the how and why, l
those. Stand on His word and lea

Unfortunately, many people today do not
see it that way. I learned a very unfortunat
so many years with mortgage loans and insurance. I did lea
to get my hopes up. Sometimes I would spend months pursuing a single prospect, or I would make more than 300 phone calls in a week just to get one sale. It was difficult to find prospective clients who were interested in meeting with me. Then I would go into the appointment with only halfway interested parties. Many times I went to the customer's home for the appointment and I would soon realize that they wanted someone to visit with them, so they could talk about their grandkids or they had just said yes to get me off the phone.

Often, they weren't even home when I got there. The one or two that were partially serious would usually draw the decision process out for months. They were constantly rescheduling or would just say that they were "still thinking about it." Eventually, I would come across someone who understood the importance of protecting their assets for their loved ones, and I would walk them through all the paperwork and sign all the forms. I would leave the house feeling relieved and go home to tell my wife that it finally closed hoping that I would finally get paid for all my hard work. Even after that, sometimes I would go into the office the next day to see a message flashing on my voicemail. Guess who is no longer interested, guess who asks if it's too late to void the transaction. Of course, it's not too late! There are too many regulations in place for that! So then I would have to go home to my loving, *usually patient* wife and tell her that no money would be coming. All that driving around, all that time spent, all the

I put out with nothing coming back. That is devastating very disappointing. Life can be that way, but thankfully that s not how God works.

It doesn't take very many disappointments for us to start losing our hope!

Naturally, I would lose interest when it took too long to make any money. It became harder and harder to keep making those phone calls and continue to drive around the town talking to people. But when, a big sale finally went through, it often made it all worthwhile. I have learned that those situations ae great parallel for our journey with God. As I felt when I first moved in with my in-laws, sometimes I felt that I was doing everything right and I still got dumped on. It's frustrating when you lose your hope. In the writing/publishing process of this book, I was discouraged many times. I have had those negative thoughts that "I just can't take it anymore, is it ever going to happen? There are too many setbacks. I should just give up. Who am I to write this stuff?" The only thing that kept me going was my vision. I knew that God anointed me to write this book, and I did not want to stand in His way! In all things, you will need to hold steady with your vision.

An excellent example of never giving up on a promise starts in Numbers 13:30 and ends in Joshua 14. You have probably heard that Moses sent the 12 spies into Canaan on a little recon mission. Caleb and Joshua were the only ones mentioned to have taken God's words to heart. They were confident that He could bring them through anything because He said so. Caleb, at the age of 40 (in Numbers 13:30, Joshua 14), stood in the face of embarrassment proclaiming that they would be able to conquer the inhabitants and take possession of their promised land Canaan just like God said. Almost everyone else saw the giants and the insurmountable obstacles. They forgot about their vision and the power of God that could move mountains. Caleb knew better and spoke up, but the people had lost faith. Caleb was faithful and stood on God's promises, but the others decided to take matters into their own hands. Maybe he never said it out loud, but certainly, he would have been expecting a great reward for his faithfulness.

Caleb's faith was rewarded with a promise that one day his family would inherit the land.

The story goes on with the Israelites being forced to wonder the desert for 40 years because of their doubt. Did you ever realize that Caleb had to wonder with them? I wonder if he felt like a child getting socks on Christmas day. Picture this great man of faith doing exactly what God expected and still finding himself among the complainers and whiners. These people doubted the very same God who had given Caleb such an incredible promise. I often try to imagine his thoughts in those years. "Has God forgotten me?" I'm sure the thought had to pass through his mind a time or two. It had to seem unfair that Caleb was trapped in a world of walking endless miles in the dirt, pitching his tent and eating manna because of other people's doubt. Certainly, he could almost taste the grapes and pomegranates and figs that he saw those people carrying in the Valley of Eshcol. Did he think about that while he was in the desert? *Caleb would turn the age of 85 before that promise would come to fruition.* According to the Bible, he was unwavering in his faith and Joshua was able to reward Caleb with the land of Hebron because of that faith. What an amazing story of patience. He waited 45 years for God to make good on His promise! I can hardly wait 45 seconds in the drive thru for my McDonald's!

I don't believe a Christian should ever lose hope.

Hope is such a vital part of the human psyche. Have you ever inadvertently crushed a child's dream by telling them they can't do something they are trying to do? (Please don't if you haven't already.) You'll soon see the disappointment cross their face. You'll see their whole demeanor change. I believe hope is important because it is so closely related to faith. Once you truly believe something, it becomes a part of you. It consumes you, and you start talking about it. I have quoted this scripture previously in this book, but I want to say it again; Proverbs 18:21, "The tongue has the power of life and death, and those who love it will eat its fruit.." *When you start talking about your vision, you start to believe it; this can impact others around you.* Soon, your actions will begin to align with your words and thoughts.

Only your doubt can get in your way. Doubt, as a noun, is "uncertainty," but, as a verb, it is so much worse. As a verb, it is "thinking something unlikely and not trusting something or someone." When you say the words, "I doubt it," you are taking ownership of that doubt; you are welcoming it and allowing it to fester in your spirit. The only thing that causes you to question is past failures (or other people's failures). You need to acquire a short memory for those failures. It's like having a bad day on the golf course and finishing with a perfect drive on the 18th hole. You can choose to complain about the ones that fell in the water (although Philippians 4:13 says not to), or you can brag to all your friends about the one perfect shot. It is up to you to think of it as a positive or negative experience. It is up to you to have hope or doubt the next time out.

Practice Point: What vision did you have that you have begun to doubt? I encourage you to stop and pray about it. If you feel that God is supporting this dream or vision, write out some scriptures that support that and put them all over your house, so you see them daily. Write down your feelings and look at it again in a few weeks to see how you're feeling about it. Repeat as necessary.

CHAPTER 10

KNOWING WHEN IT'S GOD

I USED TO HAVE perfect eyesight. One day, when I was about 25 years old, I realized that the clock on the far wall of the office where I worked was blurry. I had never really thought much about my vision before that, but suddenly, I had to get glasses. Something I had never really put any thought into before was now becoming a hindrance to me. I have worn glasses for more than ten years now, and I don't think about it too much. However, when my glasses are smudged, or I forget where I left them, I quickly remember how much I depend on those glasses working properly. Now I understand what it's like to not be able to see. I say this because there is an interesting correlation with wearing glasses and becoming ever mindful. I can go around without my glasses on, but it's very easy to miss things. When I don't have my glasses on, some things are impossible to see. *I believe when we are not intentionally aware of and focused on what God has for us; we will miss things.* We will miss opportunities when they arise. As I have to clean my glasses often, so I must rebalance my spiritual focus.

In this same way, it is imperative that we allow the Holy Spirit to convict us and draw us closer to God's voice regularly.

Growing up around Christians and being at church so much, I often heard people say "God told me..." or "The Holy Spirit put on my heart..." I've seen these people act very irrationally to the point of being completely irresponsible just because they've convinced themselves that they are doing God's work. Having close relationships with some of these people, I saw later that they were often just using these "God terms" to make themselves feel better about a selfish decision. It's very tempting to get almost narcissistic and use God's word to give you the feeling that you are operating based on faith instead of your selfish plan. That is what I want to explore in this chapter. *There is a big difference between listening and obeying.* We've discussed this a bit already, but if we plan to be mindful, we will have to prepare ourselves to take the next step. Being completely obedient to Him is much harder than simply being cognitively aware. It's easy to get to the point where we ask God before we act, but when God wants us to do something that we do not want to do, that's where the real test begins.

Throughout my work history, I have regularly had to drive a lot for work. When I was a life insurance agent and drove to clients' houses, I often enjoyed having that time to myself where I could pray and reflect on the previous day or think of what I would do that day. I always felt that it was a bit of a waste of my time, though. So, I made a CD of myself saying Bible verses that I was trying to memorize and I would listen to it on the way. It was a great idea, and it helped me in my walk with Jesus until I got a subscription to a music service on my phone. I immediately had access to thousands of songs and driving was an excellent way to listen to as many of them as possible. Soon, I stopped listening to the scripture CD and, although the music was Christian and uplifting, it was not the same. Recently, I was enjoying a new album, and then I realized that I had developed a routine of not even acknowledging God in the morning but going straight to my music. Obviously, there is nothing wrong with listening to music, especially when it's glorifying God. However, that too can be something that prevents me from hearing what God is trying to say to me. Recently, I felt convicted of this and have decided to stop and say a quick prayer first to be sure that I am mindful of what God is teaching me. Sometimes this prayer reminds me to listen to that scripture CD first. Other times, I get a release where I know it's ok to move on and listen to my music. I will admit that there are days where it takes a while before I feel that release, and I get disappointed that I have to wait. Listening for God's direction is a hard habit to make, but I have had many fantastic ideas come to mind through these times.

What I have come to believe with all my heart is that when I honor God first, He will always bless my obedience.

We have to understand that God's agenda is bigger than our own. Sometimes He will want us to listen for Him for a long time before He answers. I think that He just wants us to acknowledge Him first and be in the presence of mind where we can hear those soft, gentle nudges that would otherwise be drowned out. I am reminded of a time many years ago before I got married. I was hanging around the house with nothing to do, and I felt like God wanted me to go to the mall and witness. I was a bit nervous because that would mean plopping myself down on a bench next to some random person (that was probably just ready to go home after a long day of shopping) and breaking into an awkward conversation about Christianity. Obediently I drove to the mall and walked through the halls praying and asking who God wanted me to see. At the end of my second walkthrough, I was getting a bit upset realizing there was no one I felt to who I felt drawn. I know beyond any doubt that God said to me, "There is no one today. I just wanted to see if you would be obedient." I remember just smiling and shaking my head and going home, surprised at this test. *Please note that there have been many times where I did not follow this nudge and felt very guilty about it later.* There have been other times where I did something like that and got into really encouraging conversations. It gets addictive after a while.

I used to work in the mall at a little kiosk where I sat and sold ice cream. Almost every night I would see a guy walk through the stores with his friends. He seemed to be the leader of the pack. His baggy, sagging jeans along with his oversized shirts gave me the impression that he was some thug or gangster. *I always had the feeling that I should pray for him…so I did.* Every time I saw him walking and laughing with his friends I prayed, "God, I don't know anything about that young man, but you do. You know his situation. You know his home life. You know his future. I pray that he comes to know you and leads his friends to you." Quite a few years later I was leading a drama team at a church, and the youth pastor asked me if I had met Manny. He described Manny to me and said that he wanted to start helping in the youth group. He had just recently left the life of gangs and violence and received Christ. I was pretty excited at this point because I was really into Christian rap music and hoped we would click. When Manny got there, I immediately knew he was the same guy I had prayed for so long ago. Once again I smiled and shook my head. You can imagine how amazing it was to be able to share this story with him! I'm not saying I'm the reason Manny came to Christ, but I do believe it helped.

I believe that God will often show you the fruit of your obedience if you're looking for it.

I have to tell just one more story about this. I lived in Lafayette, Indiana for quite some time. (Boiler Up!) I used to pass by a strip club on my way to work every day. I would pray this prayer every time: "God shut that place down and use that building for your glory." I prayed that for at least two years. Then, I noticed that there was a "For Sale" sign on the building. Not long after that, it became a Christian coffee house! They even have Christian concerts there on Fridays and Saturdays and a church service on Sundays! It is called Sacred Grounds. An interesting side note is that Jeremy Camp (the Christian singer) is from Lafayette, and it is his dad that runs the church. I actually got to meet Jeremy at a concert and was able to share this story with him!

Even I have a hard time believing that I had anything to do with these events. I am okay with accepting that I didn't have anything to do with it and that it is just an interesting coincidence. *However, what if it was my prayer?* It is interesting how the more I pray, the more coincidences seem to occur. In First Corinthians 3:6-7, Paul says "I planted the seed, Apollos watered it, but God has been making it grow. So neither the one who plants nor the one who waters is anything, but only God, who makes things grow." It is pretty amazing to think that God; omniscient, omnipotent, omnipresent God who is the creator of everything, can use little ol' me to get His work done. If this is true, and He does listen to us when we pray, why would we not access this resource? I believe He does care about every little thing you are concerned with (even down to us getting a good price when we go shopping). My wife has a minor handicap, and it is difficult for her to walk long distances without assistance. As we live in Alberta, Canada and it is often snowy and cold and hard to find parking. We regularly pray for a good parking spot when we go shopping. It ALWAYS happens. People often laugh at me when I say this, but I think God enjoys blessing His people.

If there is something you're saying to God, He is listening!

It's interesting what we learn from movies and music and society. We're taught to be sad when someone dies; we're taught to be angry and vengeful when offended. We're taught that beauty only really matters when it's on the outside. If we don't completely understand something, we should be afraid of it because it may hurt us. Many of these false pretenses may have some accuracy, but it is necessary that even our emotional responses become validated through God's Word. Indeed, we need to use wisdom and adhere to good advice, but we do not have to react to situations based on our volatile emotions.

If you can grasp a better understanding of knowing when it's God speaking to you as oppose to just a random idea, you will learn not to be disappointed. Let me unpack that a bit. You are only disappointed when things do not go the way you hoped they would. When you learn to place your faith in God's direction, you learn that His plan is higher than your own. When you can honestly look around and say that you know you are doing what God wants you to do, you will get to a place where your agenda is no longer the highest priority. You will have a certain kind of peace. I am not the best at this all the time, but I am getting better. It doesn't matter what my situation or my surroundings are because I'm happy with who I am and where God is leading me.

I am satisfied with the road God is leading me down, thus when things do not go the way I want, I need to trust that He has a plan.

When you loosen the grip on your expectations, you give God permission to go to work!

When you realize that it is only your lack of faith that can limit God in your life, you will begin to align your moral compass. If you take one thing away from the reading of this book, please write this down: *Do not suppress God's will for your life by allowing your selfish desires to limit your obedience.* As a parent, I see how God must get frustrated with His children. We disobey because we think we know a better way. The right decision should be obvious (and the Holy Spirit is probably screaming it in our ear), but we are stubborn. It's like the old Twilight Zone TV shows. Generally, the character will act one way based on what he knows and at the end, he finds out he was missing something that would have made everything so much simpler. Many times we pray for someone and then get upset when God doesn't appear to be answering that prayer. We just need to learn to trust Him. When you are praying in a situation, or you feel that God may be nudging you towards something, give Him the freedom to respond in His way. Consciously ask God if your decision is what he wants you to do or how he wants you to do it.

If you do want to get better at knowing when something is a God idea (and not just a good idea); you will have to develop a real habit of giving Him your time. Maybe you are sitting in traffic on your way to work because God needs to get you alone, to get your attention. I know that life gets hectic. Many times, you are busy Monday through Friday and Saturdays are full of errand running or cleaning. I know that it can feel like Sunday is the only day off. It is necessary that we become faithful with our time (which is God's time anyway). I don't want you to go away from this book with a feeling that you can't ever rest or make your own decisions. I believe the more faithful we are to God with our time; the more we realize that giving it back to Him is not a sacrifice at all. Giving our time to help at church and being faithful with our tithes and offering simply gives God an opportunity to bless us. I believe the principal goes much deeper. It is not so much, "Does God want me to watch the TV show?" but more of a "Does He want me watch that TV show right now?"

Just because your favorite show comes on Thursday night at 9 pm doesn't mean God stops talking to you then.

Matthew 6:20 says to "store up your treasures in heaven." Recently I started buying the packs of snack size candy bars so that I can give them out randomly. It's amazing at how surprised people get and how good it makes me feel. I love leaving a small gift at the door of my daughter's bedroom, so she sees it when she gets up for school in the morning. If God created us in His image and He is a giver, then we should be givers in all areas, right? *If you start recognizing when God is putting the idea on your heart and start being obedient to that, you will find this lifestyle becoming very addictive.* It very quickly turns from something you're forcing yourself to do into something you're looking forward to doing. When you have some free time and no one bothering you, that's where your motives are tested most. What is it you choose? I know God's Word reminds us to rest, but I don't think it means to let our free time take over and become more important to us than God's time! In Malachi chapter 3, God said that He would throw open the floodgates of heaven and rebuke the devourer. I believe that, when you become a generous giver of your time (and finances), God will rebuke your devourer! However, we have to be careful not to just quote God's promises. We should back them up with obedience.

Practice Point: Are you too busy for God to speak to you? Your devotion time or church time cannot be the only time where God has the freedom to talk to you. Stop again and pray for God to reveal some things to you about your schedule. Ask Him to help you know for certain when it is Him that is speaking to you. Remember to write this down.

CHAPTER 11

DELAY BY DESIGN

IT IS NO ACCIDENT that this chapter which is largely about patience follows the chapter regarding being attentive to God speaking to you. As I talk to Christians, I find that many of us feel that God has given us a promise. It is likely that you are reading this because, at one time or another, either someone has spoken into you or God has secured something within your spirit in your prayer time. *Hopefully, you believe that there is a plan and a purpose for your life and that there is something great which you will achieve or accomplish before you leave this earth.* Many people that I have spoken to have said they are not living their lives aimlessly. God created us in a way that we want to explore and imagine and understand.

There is something inside of us that drives us and spurs us on. Often we must be reminded of God's promises as our carnal minds begin to drift. We live in such a fast-paced world that it is hard to continue believing something if it does not happen quickly. It doesn't help when our adversary spits his venom of doubt at us every time we turn around. This is why it's so important to remind yourself of your promise and memorize Bible scriptures that support it. This way, you have ammunition to fire back as soon as the Satan rears his ugly head. If you want this book to change your life, you must remember that His ways are higher than ours, and we cannot get upset at Him when He moves slower than we would like Him to move.

I believe God knows not only the plan for each of our lives but also the timeline that will be most beneficial.

Rushing God's plan is tempting. If you took the previous chapter seriously, you are likely getting excited about a word that God has put into your spirit. If you are practicing and indeed becoming ever mindful about how God wants to speak *to* you, *through* you, and *around* you, it's easy to get eager. Unfortunately, eagerness may lead to impatience, which may result in making a terrible mistake (as we will explore in this chapter). When God's promise for your life seems to be delayed, you should respond in one of the following ways:

GO TO your prayer closet: Ask if this is still God's promise for you at this stage in your life. (Is it a trust issue or a timing issue?)

GO TO God's Word: What does the Bible say about your situation, dream, or promise?

GO TO a trusted Christian friend: Sometimes we need to talk things out, and we realize that it was a ridiculous idea in the first place, OR we are missing something.

If you are earnestly seeking God's plan, at some point, you will have peace in your spirit about this direction. If I remember correctly, part of the fruit of the Spirit is "peace" (Galatians 5:22). Jesus said, "Peace I leave with you; my peace I give you. I do not give to you as the world gives. Do not let your hearts be troubled and do not be afraid" in John 14:27. Trust yourself and your God enough that if you are on the wrong path, there will be warning signs. When you see those, go back and ask God. God is a God of peace (1 Corinthians 14:33), and He does not want to trick you.

Do not mistake delay for something being wrong.

Imagine God promises you that He will make many nations out of your family. Your children will begin a legacy that will change the course of many nations to come. There is one huge problem, though. Your spouse is unable to give you a child. To make it worse, you are both getting up there in years and having a child at this point may seem ridiculous. God's promised outcome seems unlikely, to say the least. However, you know God can do anything He says, so you believe Him. You pick up and move because He tells you to do so. Now you're all by yourself with nothing except a promise. I'm sure by now you've realized that I'm speaking of Abraham and Sarah from the book of Genesis. These small beginnings are the perfect scenario for a beautiful story, but there are a few things in this story that are not so beautiful, right? I assure you we haven't come as far as we should have in learning from the lessons that Abraham experienced. Although this happened thousands of years ago, the story is still a strong parallel to our lives as modern-day Christians.

Their names are Abram and Sarai at the beginning of this story. Abram was the ripe, ol' age of 70 when we first read of God's promise in Genesis 12. *As any of us do when we first get a word from God, Abram got a new lease on life (maybe he even felt a goose bump or two).* He suddenly found himself with a new-found joie de vive. He excitedly told his wife and bravely led the way into this new life. A new life full of unbelievable favor and blessings around every corner seemed to be around the corner.

Nothing would stop them now! However, within five years, he would already have to be reminded what God told him. I always thought it was kind of funny that Abram decided he must tell God that he has no children yet (Genesis 15:2). I can just picture God whispering to the Holy Spirit beside Him, "He just doesn't get it, does he." God proceeds to lay out exactly how this picture will end and talks to Abram as though four generations have already come and gone. Maybe this perked up Abram's spirits a bit, but ten years after this divine intervention, still no children. There was still no physical evidence to suggest that God would come through. Understandably, Sarai and Abram were getting frustrated and impatient, and that spurred them on to make the worst decision of their lives.

They took matters into their own hands (as many of us do when the hands of time are moving faster that we would like) and it did not end well.

We know that when Abram, Sarai, and Hagar (Sarai's handmade) made the decision to come up with their plan and carry that plan out, they created a real problem. There was immediate tension between Sarai and Hagar. We hear nothing for 13 years. Although what they did was very reasonable for the time and perfectly acceptable, it was not God's plan. *If becoming ever mindful means anything, it means knowing that we must, MUST learn to keep God's will and timing at the forefront of every decision we make.* They had baby Ishmael when Abram was age 86 (Genesis 16:16), but this would not serve to answer God's promise for their lives. Finally, in Genesis 17, God changes the names to Abraham and Sarah and restates His promise. God opens Sarah's womb, and she gave birth to Isaac the next year. Have you ever wondered what would have happened if Abraham had continued to trust God and not "hurried" the plan along? I guess some of the world conflicts we see today would not have happened (as there would never have been the Ishmaelites or their association with the Amalekites and Moabites). This is just my theory of course, but I also wonder if they might have had Isaac a lot sooner. Now, think of how you may have done something very similar.

Now, it's very easy to question how they could get their eyes off God's promises (especially now that we know the rest of the story), but take heed to a lesson well learned. Peter warned us, "But do not forget this one thing, dear friends: With the Lord a day is like a thousand years, and a thousand years are like a day. The Lord is not slow in keeping his promise, as some understand slowness. Instead he is patient with you, not wanting anyone to perish, but everyone to come to repentance." (2 Peter 3:8+9). *The promises God has given you are not tarnished by the years of waiting.* We may never know why God waits so long, but if we are going to step out in faith, we must also have the faith to trust His timing.

Are there areas in your life where you are trying to speed up His plan?

I believe God's delay is by His design. He knows exactly when you will be ready for His particular purpose. Let's say you wanted to make a delicious cherry pie. You get a recipe and gather all the ingredients. You decide even to make the crust yourself, so you roll it all out. You go to the best local farmer's market and find the most beautiful, perfectly ripe cherries (hopefully from British Columbia). Next, you measure out all the ingredients correctly. Finally, it's all put together, and you can almost taste it. As it's cooking in the oven, the heavenly aromas fill the house. The recipe tells you to bake it for about 45 minutes and just 10 minutes into it, you begin to imagine what it will look like on your plate with some vanilla ice cream. You just can't stand it anymore, so you decide just to take it out early, slop it on your plate, and dig in. It's not going to taste right, is it? Even though you do all that work and go through all that trouble to prepare it perfectly, if you take it out of the oven before it's time, the pie will not taste right. It will not come out the way you've imagined. It may look right but it won't taste right. Since it was used before its designated time, it did not live up to its potential. We are all like cherry pies in God's oven. God knows how He put your life together and only He knows exactly when you are ready for His purpose. We may never understand all His reasons, but we owe it to Him to let the journey play out.

Trust Him enough to believe His promises for you no matter how long it takes, no matter how tough it may get.

Practice Point: Do you feel you have been waiting too long for a promise? Becoming ever mindful is all about trusting God's timing. Ask God if you have missed something or if you are supposed to trust His plan still. I believe He will give you a spirit of piece regarding the timing of your promise!

CHAPTER 12

PUTTING IT ALL TOGETHER

WE'RE ALMOST DONE. IF you have been taking this seriously, you might be wondering, "now what?" Through this journey, from becoming aware of what God is trying to tell you all the way to stating your vision and waiting patiently, it can become very self-oriented. That's not the whole picture, though. *Once this becomes a part of you, it should spill over into nearly everything you do.* I believe the absolute most important part of becoming ever mindful is that we become witnesses for Christ.

NEWSFLASH: We are adults now, IT *IS* OK TO TALK TO STRANGERS!

The term "witnessing" can sometimes bring up negative emotions. Maybe you have experienced someone preaching a message of judgment on a street corner (probably offering "free" food to hook you in). Maybe you saw a church group forcing Bible tracts into everyone's hand (which were immediately thrown away). Perhaps you have attempted to go door-to-door to tell people about Jesus (and received negative reactions). Regardless, you may have a sour taste in your mouth about witnessing. Let me simplify it for you.

Telling people about what Jesus Christ has done for you should never be forced.

Think of it like telling people about a vacation that you recently took. It starts out very light and relational. If the other person is interested, they will ask for more details. Maybe they ask to see the pictures or share a similar story. If they are not too interested, or if something they want to talk about is more important at the time, they move on. That's okay. You don't keep going back to what you want to say about the trip; you move along with the conversation. *You wait for the right opportunity to tell your story.* Granted, you will be eager to tell your story if it has become a part of you but that does not give you permission to go tackling people and force-feeding them. In my job, I have a lot of volunteers that want to get involved with ending homelessness. Often, they have their own ideas on evangelism and end up pushing people away. To combat this, I encourage them to "earn the right to be heard." Please do not take this for me saying to be reserved. We should take advantage of every opportunity to share our story. I just feel it is more impactful when we tell it in smaller, bite-sized pieces and allow that conversation to come about organically.

If you are not sharing your faith story at all, you may want to think about why that is.

Before what is commonly known as the Great Commission (in Matthew 28 which is AFTER Christ's resurrection) Jesus gathered His disciples together and anointed them to give them authority. I have credentials through a Pentecostal organization; so it's fun to quote that first part. However, His words quickly came with a warning that this would not be easy. There is an inherent responsibility to go to the "lost sheep" to proclaim the gospel. As you read Matthew 10, you should quickly realize that

Jesus was warning His disciples of the difficulties which declaring the gospel would bring. There would be significant resistance, and it would challenge these men to re-evaluate their priorities in life. My favorite part is that Jesus was quick to remind them that each of them was an invaluable member of God's family and that He would provide their essential needs. Fast forward to First Corinthians 13 (the love chapter which is commonly read at weddings) and you will see that Paul is talking vastly about how you must back up your actions with the spirit of love. When Jesus was preparing His disciples for His leaving, He told them to LOVE. He didn't say it would be easy. He only said to do it.

It will take work, but everyone who calls themselves a Christian has a duty to sharing their faith.

When is the last time that you actually shared your faith? I know it can sound (and be) scary. It does not have to be an intimidating situation. Acts 4:13 records that, "When they saw the courage of Peter and John and realized that they were unschooled, ordinary men, they were astonished and they took note that these men had been with Jesus." Peter and John were merely living the changed, Christian life in front of others. *When you learn to walk with Jesus every day and become ever mindful of what His mission is for your life in each moment, you will become lovingly bold.* Jesus was not a pushover, but He was also not running around stopping people in the streets to pass out Bible tracts. Instead, He was always putting Himself in a position where His day could be interrupted. Then, He would have an opportunity to intervene in someone's life. That's when the deliberate, active approach to discipleship began. He never pried into people's lives. He started with a simple conversation. He earned the right to be heard. You will act as He would, and people will see that. Going back to the vacation analogy; I WANT TO share my experience with people. That comes naturally. It is the same way with being a witness for Jesus. A simple way to start is to ask for permission to pray with someone when they share something with you. (It's okay if they say no.)

We can't go into a conversation assuming that the other person needs anything. (Maybe they do and just have not realized it yet, but you cannot lead with that.) When I used to sell life insurance, I didn't just sit down at the table, say that the client needed an individual product, and then force it on them. I started with a conversation about sports or the weather. When the time was right, I explained my purpose. I asked questions. I listened and used other informational guides so they could see where their protection shortfalls were, based on their individual needs and plans. I used their answers so they could understand their solutions. If they wanted to debate that need, they were only arguing against their answers. I learned valuable "witnessing" tips from this process.

We need to show the unchurched WHY they would want God first.

When the conversation goes deeper, you can then help them understand what sin is and how it is hurting them. I have been to and worked for many churches that are struggling with attendance or finances or even their mission. Why does this happen? Why do some seem churches always seem to be in a "transitional phase"? I am all for sticking around and believing for the best and holding on to ride through the storm, but eventually, you have to re-evaluate your methodology.

In first Samuel 4, the Philistines captured the ark, Eli died, and Phinehas' wife named her newborn son Ichabod. "She named the boy Ichabod, saying, 'The Glory has departed from Israel'—because of the capture of the ark of God and the deaths of her father-in-law and her husband. She said, 'The Glory has departed from Israel, for the ark of God has been captured'" (verses 21 and 22 NIV). Has the glory of God left your church? Has that glory left your own life? If you are not regularly telling your faith story; stop and think about why that may be.

Use this book to bring you back to a place where you are absolutely in love with Jesus and you will see positive changes naturally occur.

Being a Christian is so much more than going to church to sing a few songs, listening to three good points, and then going home. Why aren't we walking the streets talking to people (not necessarily with an evangelistic agenda)? Do we invite the community to our potluck dinners just to bless them (again, no agenda)? We need to ask the community again and again and again. Once you get to know them a bit, follow up. Remember the things they tell you, so you have more to talk about next time. When you get to know them a bit, ask some tougher questions. Maybe ask them how their walk with God is going. I believe we owe it to our community to stay interested in their lives. We have a responsibility to educate ourselves so that we are ready to witness. We can't just take the easy road and be happy that we are Christians. *Don't be a selfish Christian!*

Practice Point: Here's your chance to practice what you've learned. Write out a few sentences as to why you believe. What is your story? Why are you a Christian? What has God done for you? Look for an opportunity this week to begin sharing that story with someone. (It will take practice.)

CONCLUSION

Well, that's all for now. Becoming ever mindful is meant to be an unassuming idea that can revolutionize your daily routine. It is my prayer that this book would give you another tool in your tool belt of faith. I realize that I have not said anything extremely new or incredibly dynamic, but it is my story. It is my journey which I feel may be able to encourage others. Because of what we have gone through, my wife, Kerri and I believe God will get us through whatever trial we face. Whether we are in our darkest hour or a moment of glory, we will give God the praise and trust Him for wisdom. Our vision is to believe that God will keep our desires in line with His. We are believing for God to better our lives financially and spiritually and will use our lives for Him in whatever way possible. Our faith is more than just a good idea; it's more than a nice thing to discuss. It is a lifestyle. We will choose to be happy. My prayer in every circumstance is that God will change me, change my situation, or use my situation and I will be joyful either way. I thank you for joining me on this journey and pray that you too become ever mindful in love, faithfulness, and obedience.

Please follow this blog at becomingevermindful.wordpress.com and get involved in the discussions. I know we can all learn from each other as "iron sharpens iron." (Proverbs 27:17)

I would be honored to speak at your church or gathering and have adapted this book so that it can be used as a small group training session. Feel free to contact me through Facebook.com/becomingevermindful.

May God bless your journey!

In Christ,

David J. Sacerich

CPSIA information can be obtained
at www.ICGtesting.com
Printed in the USA
LVOW10s0031140217
524164LV00001B/2/P